♈

By the same author

Teri King's Complete Guide to Your Stars
Teri King's Astrological Horoscopes for 2004:

Taurus 20 April to 20 May
Gemini 21 May to 20 June
Cancer 21 June to 21 July
Leo 22 July to 22 August
Virgo 23 August to 22 September
Libra 23 September to 22 October
Scorpio 23 October to 21 November
Sagittarius 22 November to 21 December
Capricorn 22 December to 20 January
Aquarius 21 January to 18 February
Pisces 19 February to 19 March

Teri King's Astrological
Horoscopes for 2004

Aries

Teri King's complete horoscope
for all those whose birthdays fall
between 20 March and 19 April

Teri King

Element
An Imprint of HarperCollins*Publishers*
77–85 Fulham Palace Road
Hammersmith, London W6 8JB

The website address is: www.thorsonselement.com

and *Element* are trademarks of
HarperCollins*Publishers* Limited

First published 2003

1 3 5 7 9 10 8 6 4 2

© Teri King 2003

Teri King asserts the moral right to be
identified as the author of this work

A catalogue record for this book
is available from the British Library

ISBN 0 00 714777 5

Printed in Great Britain by
Clays Ltd, St Ives plc

All rights reserved. No part of this publication may be
reproduced, stored in a retrieval system, or transmitted,
in any form or by any means, electronic, mechanical,
photocopying, recording or otherwise, without the prior
permission of the publishers.

Contents

Introduction **vii**

How Does Astrology Work? **1**

The Sun in Aries **4**

The Year Ahead: Overview **8**

Career Year **10**

Money Year **12**

Love and Sex Year **15**

Health and Diet Year **19**

Numerology Year **23**

Your Sun Sign Partner **45**

Your Child of the Zodiac **61**

Monthly and Daily Guides **63**

Aries
20 March to 19 April

Ruling Planet: **Mars**
Element: **Fire**
Qualities: **Masculine, Positive**
Planetary Principle: **Action**
Primal Desire: **Leadership**
Colour: **Red**
Jewels: **Amethyst, Diamond**
Day: **Sunday**
Magical Number: **Five**

Famous Aries
Henry Kissinger, Warren Beatty, Julie Christie, Marlon Brando, Steve McQueen, Tennessee Williams, Harry Houdini, Joan Crawford, Bette Davis, Joseph Pulitzer, Vincent Van Gogh, Nikita Kruschev, John Major.

Introduction

Astrology has many uses, not least of these its ability to help us to understand both ourselves and other people. Unfortunately there are many misconceptions and confusions associated with it, such as that old chestnut – how can a zodiac forecast be accurate for all the millions of people born under one particular sign?

The answer to this is that all horoscopes published in newspapers, books and magazines are, of necessity, of a general nature. Unless an astrologer can work from the date, time and place of your birth, the reading given will only be true for the typical member of your sign.

For instance, let's take a person born on 9 August. This person is principally a subject of Leo, simply because the Sun occupied that section of the heavens known as Leo during 22 July to 22 August.* However, when delving into astrology at its most serious, there are other influences that need to be taken into consideration – for example, the Moon. This planet enters a fresh sign every 48 hours. On the birth date in question

---

* Because of the changing position of the planets, calendar dates for astrological signs change from year to year.

it may have been in, say, Virgo. And if this were the case it would make our particular subject Leo (Sun representing willpower) and Virgo (Moon representing instincts) or, if you will, a Leo/Virgo. Then again, the rising sign of 'ascendant' must also be taken into consideration. This also changes constantly as the Earth revolves: approximately every two hours a new section of the heavens comes into view – a new sign passes over the horizon. The rising sign is of the utmost importance, determining the image projected by the subject to the outside world – in effect, the personality.

The time of birth is essential when compiling a birth chart. Let us suppose that in this particular instance Leo was rising at the time of birth. Now, because two of the three main influences are Leo, our sample case would be fairly typical of his or her sign, possessing all the faults and attributes associated with it. However, if the Moon and ascendant had been in Virgo then, whilst our subject would certainly display some of the Leo attributes or faults, it is more than likely that for the most part he or she would feel and behave more like a Virgoan.

As if life weren't complicated enough, this procedure must be carried through to take into account all the remaining planets. The position and signs of Mercury, Venus, Mars, Jupiter, Saturn, Uranus, Neptune and Pluto must all be discovered, plus the aspect formed from one planet to another. The calculation and interpretation of these movements by an astrologer will then produce an individual birth chart.

Because the heavens are constantly changing, people with identical charts are a very rare occurrence. Although it is not inconceivable that it could happen, this would mean that the two subjects were born not only on the same date and at the same time, but also in the same place. Should such an incident occur, then the deciding factors as to how these individuals would differ in their approach to life, love, career, financial prospects and so on, would be due to environmental and parental influence.

Returning to our hypothetical Leo: our example with the rising Sun in Leo and Moon in Virgo, may find it useful not only to read up on his or her Sun sign (Leo) but also to read the section dealing with Virgo (the Moon). Nevertheless, this does not invalidate Sun sign astrology. This is because of the great power the Sun possesses, and on any chart this planet plays an important role.

Belief in astrology does not necessarily mean believing in totally determined lives – that we are predestined and have no control over our fate. What it does clearly show is that our lives run in cycles, for both good and bad and, with the aid of astrology, we can make the most of, or minimize, certain patterns and tendencies. How this is done is entirely up to the individual. For example, if you are in possession of the knowledge that you are about to experience a lucky few days or weeks, then you can make the most of them by pushing ahead with plans. You can also be better prepared for illness, misfortune, romantic upset and every adversity.

Astrology should be used as it was originally intended – as a guide, especially to character. In this direction it is invaluable and it can help us in all aspects of friendship, work and romance. It makes it easier for us to see ourselves as we really are and, what's more, as others see us. We can recognize both our own weaknesses and strengths and those of others. It can give us both outer confidence and inner peace.

In the following pages you will find: personality profiles; an in-depth look at the year ahead from all possible angles, including numerology; Monthly and Daily guides; and your

Sun sign partner guide – plus a brief section on your child of the Zodiac, for those with children born under this sign.

Used wisely, astrology can help you through life. It is not intended to encourage complacency, since, in the final analysis, what you do with your life is up to you. This book will aid you in adopting the correct attitude to the year ahead and thus maximize your chances of success. Positive thinking is encouraged because this helps us to attract positive situations. Allow astrology to walk hand-in-hand with you and you will be increasing your chances of success and happiness.

How Does Astrology Work?

You often hear people say that there is no scientific explanation of astrology. This is not a very scientific thing to say because, in fact, astrological calculations may be explained in a very precise way and they can be done by anyone with a little practice and some knowledge of the movement of stars and planets. However, the interpretations and conclusions drawn from these observations are not necessarily consistent or verifiable, and, to be sure, predicted events do not always happen. Yet astrology has lasted in our culture for over 3,000 years, so there must be something in it!

So how can we explain that astrology? Well, along with your individual birth sign goes a set of deep-seated characteristics and an understanding of these can give you fresh insights into why you behave as you do. Reading an astrological interpretation, even if it is just to find out how, say, a new relationship might develop, means that you should think about yourself in a very deep way. But it is important to remember that the stars don't determine your fate. It is up to you to use them to the best advantage in any situation.

Although astrology, like many other 'alternative' subjects, such as homoeopathy, dowsing and telepathy, cannot completely be explained, there have been convincing experiments to show that it is right far more often than chance would allow. The best-known studies are those of the French statistician, Michel Gauqueline, whose results were checked by a professor at the University of London who declared, grudgingly, that 'there was something in it'.

An important aspect of astrology is to look at how the Sun and the Moon affect that natural world around us, day-in-day-out. For instance, the rise and fall of the tides is purely a result of the movement and position of the Moon relative to the Earth. If this massive magnetic pull can move the oceans of the Earth, what does it do to us? After all, we are, on average, over 60 per cent water!

When it comes to the ways in which the Sun may change the world, a whole book could be written about it. Of the influences we know about, there is length of day, heat, light, solar storms, and magnetic, ultra-violet and many other forms of radiation. And all this from over 90 million miles away! For example, observation of birds has shown that before migration – governed by the changing length of the days – birds put on extra layers of fat, and also they experience a nocturnal restlessness shortly before setting off on their travels. I'm not suggesting that we put on weight and experience sleepless nights because of the time of year, but many people will tell you that different seasons affect them in different ways.

Also in the natural world, there is a curious species of giant worm that lives in underground caverns in the South Pacific. Twice a year, as the Sun is rising and the tide is at its highest, these worms come to the surface of the ocean. The inhabitants of the islands considered them a great delicacy! There are so many instances where the creatures of this planet respond to the influences of the Moon and the Sun that it is only sensible to wonder whether the position of other planets also has an effect, even if it is subtler and less easy to identify.

Finally, we come to the question as to how astrology might work in predicting future events? As we have seen, the planetary bodies are likely to affect us in all sorts of ways, both physically and mentally. Most often, subtle positions in the planets will make slight changes in our emotional states and, of course, this determines how we behave. By drawing up a chart based on precise birth times, and by using their intuition, some astrologers can make precise observations about how influences in the years ahead are likely to shape the life of an individual. Many people are very surprised at how well an astrologer seems to 'understand' them after reading a commentary on their birth chart!

More strange are the astrologers who appear to be able to predict future events, ages before they happen. The most famous example of all is the 16th-century French astrologer, Nostradamus, who is well-known for having predicted the possibility of world destruction at the end of the last millennium. Don't worry; I think I can cheerfully put everyone's mind at rest by assuring you that the world will go on for a good many years yet. Although Nostradamus certainly made some very accurate predictions in his life-time, his prophecies for our future are very obscure and are hotly disputed by all the experts. Mind you, it is quite clear that there are likely to be massive changes ahead. It is a possibility, for instance, that information may come to light about past civilizations, now sunk under the Mediterranean Sea. This could give us a good idea about how people once lived in the past, and pointers as to how we should live in the future. Try not to fear, dear reader. Astrology is a tool for us to use; if we use it wisely, no doubt we will survive with greater wisdom and with a greater respect for our world and each other.

The Sun in Aries

The Sun in Aries produces a physically distinctive type of person. Though a pure Aries is probably non-existent because of the hereditary factor and other planetary considerations, all those born between 20 March and 19 April who have Aries ascendant, which will apply if you were born around the dawn, will be fairly typical of your sign. Maybe you will have marked features, such as bushy eyebrows, or a dip at the bridge of the nose forming the sign of the Ram. The ram, of course, is an animal whose main means of defence or attack is by butting, and Rams certainly utilize this power metaphorically, if not literally!

Your progress in life is by means of attack. You lower your head and charge – a simple and effective tactic, but rather hard on the head. Because of your impatience and Ram-like impulsiveness, you could be somewhat accident-prone. Sooner or later you'll end up injuring your face or head. Aries children are especially vulnerable, and adults frequently carry some sort of scar commemorating an early introduction to their Ram-like nature. Burns, scalds and cuts are regular woes.

A typical Aries doesn't give his/her body much chance to accumulate fat. You often walk very slightly bent, as though

The Sun in Aries

leading with your head, which, of course, is used as a battering ram. Occasionally there is something pugnacious and belligerent about you; you emanate an irritating air about you that sometimes upsets the more sensitive members of the zodiac.

You are incredibly self-confident, convinced that you can do anything that appeals to you better than the next person. Experience is something you believe you are born with. If you don't know a subject or a technique, you will read up on it, or ask. You are an exceptionally good listener and you want to learn. But all the time you are waiting – with good-humoured impatience – to leap in whenever you see a gap in the conversation.

You learn quickly because you can't bear the thought of someone else being in a position to give you orders. Wherever you work, you'll end up making decisions immediately, or ably implementing a policy that has been laid down. But this is a speciality of yours – impressing the guys at the top. You have no objection either to some faceless boss way up in his ivory tower handing down broad objectives. But don't let him, or his sidekicks, try to tell you how you go about achieving them – you'll quit first!

Fortunately you get your own little number going. What impresses employers about you is your eager willingness and get up and go-ness. No-one could ever call you lazy – silly, perhaps, immature, and foolish at times – but never lazy. If the boss would only leave you to your own devices, you'll promise him the world and worry about fulfilling your promises at a later date. Well, you can't have everything I suppose.

Not surprisingly you are unquenchably self-confident, which often lands you in a jam. There are limits and you just won't acknowledge when someone throws down a challenge. Say yes, pay later, is the Aries motto.

Another remarkable thing is the way you put a story together that will convince even the most hard-headed tycoon that you're just the person for the job. You're frequently not qualified for the work you do, but your manner is so persuasive and convincing that others find it impossible to believe you could be so self-assured without having all the necessary training. You're the type who in Wild West days would have accepted a gun duel and learned to shoot on the way to the appointment.

Where your job is concerned you have the knack of making important decisions when nobody else is around. You assume responsibility in a shockingly irresponsible way. You'll make an off-the-cuff decision without the boss's authority just because he is at lunch. Nevertheless, despite all of this, others find it difficult to resist you, and your winning ways break down the most determined opposition around you.

When it comes to love you are equally impetuous, and both sexes are happy to do the wooing and pursuing. But you do get bored easily and you need a partner who can match your sense of fun and adventure and who can also handle your temper. You never shy away from a fight but you don't bear a grudge. In fact, you sincerely believe that a good argument with plenty of plate-throwing is a healthy release of tension. After all, it's so much fun making up afterwards, isn't it? You definitely need a partner who can stand up to you. Sensitive types might not last very long with you, either because you scare them away or because once you've turned them into putty in your hands, you completely lose interest. After all, there is always someone new to launch your charm

The Sun in Aries

offensive on. Once you have made your mind up, however, you can be a faithful partner and touchingly child-like in your affections.

The Year Ahead: Overview

During 2004 Pluto continues its way through the fiery sign of Sagittarius, and this is the area of your chart that tends to rule matters related to further education and travel. Whenever Pluto is well aspected you will find temporary relief, but when the more negative side to this planet surfaces, and planet is in retrograde movement from March all the way through to August, oh dear, you may feel that you're running into one stumbling block and obstacle after another. When this occurs the best thing to do is to turn your attention elsewhere until you receive some kind of 'go ahead' from the stars.

Neptune, too, will be residing in the same sign for the entire year, and that is in the sign of Aquarius. When this is well starred you find added inspiration, which will help you to achieve all your goals. But when it is badly aspected, confusion, muddle and deception are possibilities, and you must take care.

That eccentric and sometimes exciting planet, Uranus, will be in Pisces for the entire year. That's a rather secretive area of your chart and because of this strain and tension may be below the surface from time to time. Make sure that you get

The Year Ahead: Overview

yourself organized because failure to do so could mean that you are 'shown up' on the working front, and you know how sensitive that ego of yours is, and this is something you seriously need to avoid if at all possible. Whenever Uranus moves into retrograde movement, which you can check out by the Monthly and Daily Guides, you must take extra care. If you dash ahead in your usual fashion, you'll become seriously unstuck.

That planet we all love to hate – Saturn – will be in Cancer for the entire year, so it might be a good idea to double check in the Monthly and Daily Guides as to when it is in retrograde movement, or when behaving itself. However, at least Saturn can steady us, and as long as you proceed carefully this planet will hold no fear for you.

What about Jupiter? It is always known for being lucky, but alas this isn't strictly true. Well, it is situated in Virgo until 24 September, so up until this date you'd be wise to listen to the advice of colleagues on the working front. They mean well, and they are not by any manner of means trying to undermine your efforts. Stand still then, and listen and there's nothing for you to worry about at all. Later on, good luck will occur through other people, because Jupiter moves on into Libra on 25 September, where it stays for the remainder of the year.

Don't be too 'pig headed' then; listen to advice that is handed on, as there's going to be a great deal of sense in what others are saying. If you fail to take heed, I'm afraid you'll be making life considerably harder for yourself than is absolutely necessary, but, of course, it is entirely up to you.

Career Year

As far as you are concerned, if success doesn't count, then you really don't know what does. What you want most out of life is to be at the top of whatever you take on board, and you are prepared to put in a lot of hard work and slog to improve your position. Success is important to you, because without it you can't really feel very good about yourself. You're relentless in your struggle for achievement. In the process you may drive yourself, and everybody around you, completely potty – although you are unlikely to even notice this.

Yours, of course, is the sign of the warrior and the pioneer, and a nice safe job is unlikely to appeal to you. Engineering, politics, exploration, mechanics or professional sports do appeal, as does any field where you can use your initiative and enterprise. Many born under this sign become successful working for themselves and, although you may fail repeatedly, this will not stop you from trying again and again, until you at least have been able to create a viable and active organization.

But what about the year ahead?

Well, when trying to find some good times where professional matters are concerned, it might be a good idea to look at Jupiter, which is going to be in Virgo until 24 September. That's the area of your chart devoted to health, which is going to be excellent, and daily routine on the working front, which is going to present you with plenty of opportunities to 'better yourself'; it's up to you to be ready to take advantage.

On 25 September Jupiter will be moving into Libra where it stays for the remainder the year. Libra, for you, seems to represent partnerships. Therefore, try not to be too single minded; listen to the advice and suggestions of other people and you'll do yourself a considerable amount of good. However, being such a fiery ambitious soul, you may not take kindly to this advice, but failure to do so could mean that there'll be a great deal of trouble for the remainder of the year and you will only have yourself to blame, so take care.

Overall, however, if you can play your astrological cards in the right order, then there's no reason why you shouldn't enjoy an extremely successful year.

Money Year

When it comes to cash, you can be quite impossible – one minute playing the miser and the next making outrageous gambles. You must remember that you tend to be too impulsive where money matters are concerned, and that that love of luxury you have tends to make a big hole in your bank account!

If you are a certain kind of Ram, then your bills will bring people knocking at your door, which you don't much like. When things get bad you have a way of refusing to confront matters. Maybe you'll go to sleep and ignore the situation, hoping that it will solve itself in some way (which, of course, it won't).

Because Taurus is in your second house in your chart, and in the money area of your life, you would ideally like to have the sense of security that money brings you. But, unlike the Bull, you don't get any satisfaction from accumulating possessions. Basically, you know that money provides you with the freedom to do what you want, when you want to, and how you want to. You like to think that at any moment you could just pick up and emigrate, or go on a luxury holiday. This isn't very practical, I think you'll agree.

What about the year ahead?

Well, the planet that represents money for you is that rather attractive planet called Venus. During January, up until the 14th anyway, Venus will be in Aquarius, which is the area of your chart devoted to friends and acquaintances, so it's definitely going to be a case of who you know and not what you know which is going to be important. However, Venus will be moving on into Pisces on the 15th and that's the area of your chart which is devoted to your instincts and what is going on behind the scenes, so you need to stay alert in these areas if you are to make the most of what is in store for you. Furthermore, you'll be making some very 'canny' purchases that will probably be the envy of your friends, who perhaps have not been quite so clever and this can't be bad.

During February your money planet, Venus, continues in Pisces until the 8th when it moves into your sign of Aries. Where cash matters are concerned you will have a happy knack of picking up on other people's vibes and helping them to make the most of their finances which, of course, will indirectly rub off on you – and this is all to the good.

Venus continues in Aries for the first five days of March, and after this moves into the earthy sign of Taurus. That's the area of your chart that represents buying and selling and short trips. All of these are likely to be successful and will help swell your bank account, which will make your bank manager smile quite considerably.

Venus continues in Taurus until 4 April when it will be moving into Gemini. People born under this sign could be lucky for you and, as long as they don't intend to blow all their hard-earned savings on a three-legged horse, then you should listen to what they have to say.

Venus continues in Gemini for an indecently long time, which is good news for you, isn't it? However, on 7 August

Venus finally moves on into Cancer and because of this it may be people at home who will be gaining although, of course, their good luck is likely to rub off on you too.

Venus remains in Cancer until 7 September when it moves into Leo – the area of your chart devoted to calculated risks, creative matters and also, to a degree, your love life. This may somehow be intertwined with finances, which seems rather promising! This kind of luck is likely to continue into October, so do stay alert.

On 4 October, Venus will be moving into Virgo and it's tips that are handed on on the working front that will be extremely useful to you, so do stay on top of what is going on.

On 29 October, Venus moves into Libra and that, of course, is your opposite sign, so quite clearly you are gaining through the thoughts and ideas of other people and, to a degree, romance – which can't be bad. Be prepared, then, to take chances in these areas whenever they crop up.

On 23 November Venus will be moving into Scorpio and because of this it wouldn't be a bad idea to go and visit your bank manager, especially if you have any cash hanging around which could be invested wisely for you. Bank managers and all figures of authority are likely to be lucky for you until 17 December, when Venus will be moving into Sagittarius for the remainder of the year. Sagittarius is a sign which represents long-distance travelling so you may be receiving some good news from friends who are abroad who may possibly be putting a good thing your way. Do stay alert and trust your old friends, because they will not guide you wrong.

Love and Sex Year

Well there's no doubt about it, Aries, when it comes to love and sex you can be something of a mystery. For a person who is fiercely independent, dramatic and daring, it often comes as a surprise to other people that you're 100 per cent in love with the drama of an exciting new face, as well as a smouldering flirtation and a larger-than-life love. Even so, even if you don't want to admit it, you want to be swept off your feet by some gorgeous member of the opposite sex and somebody who needs as much variety and excitement as you do, because excitement builds up your ego and makes you feel good about yourself.

Yes, Aries, you're the sort of person who wants to see fireworks and be generally in the forefront of any excitement going on. You're far more attracted to the aspects of romance rather than to a commitment for better or worse. You want a love life that is dreamy and never stale, with a constant array of beautiful faces that appear on your scene so that you don't become bored or jaded. You don't really believe that you can just find one love that is perfect for you, instead you live for the moment when you can open yourself up to any exciting possibility that grabs your attention.

Unfortunately you are attracted to the rather flashy sort who boasts so many accomplishments that you'll never be worried about being a loser. Regrettably, if you fall for the right line every single time, you'll only live to regret it at a later date. What you want is to be devastated by a romantic admirer. However, you simply have to settle for somebody else who is less glamorous and this deflates your ego.

Well, what about the year ahead?

Well, that planet of love, Venus, is the one we have to look to when it comes to partnership affairs. Venus will be in Aquarius until 14 January, so anything can happen and probably will. You're not going to be drawn to your usual type, rather somebody who is a little bit 'different'. However, Mars, your ruling planet is in your own sign all month, so those hormones are really tearing along through your veins and you may wonder what on earth has come over you. Others may be amused and may stand in the background smiling, which won't please you at all should you discover this. But then again, you're probably too busy to notice.

From 15 January, Venus moves into Pisces and as this is a rather secretive part of your chart, you may become embroiled in a passionate encounter which you have to keep to yourself. Do please bear in mind that if this person has someone tucked away at home, or if, heaven forbid, you yourself do, it could all end in tears. Don't say I haven't warned you!

Venus bursts into your own sign on 9 February and you will be looking good and feeling fine. You may be more inclined to compromise than to keep obstinately doing your own thing. Your friends and loved ones will be breathing a huge sigh of relief, I can assure you. And others can't help but be attracted to you at this time, so that's good news, isn't it?

Between 6 March and 3 April, Venus will be in Taurus and the financial area of your chart. You may find that romance becomes rather an expensive business and if you aren't sure about someone's honesty you should drop him or her like the proverbial hot potato. You don't mind spending money, but you hate to be taken for a fool.

On 4 April, Venus moves into Gemini, where it will remain for a very long time, in fact right up until 7 August. For most of this time you should find that brothers and sisters and your neighbours are the most delightful company. However, the planet decides, for reasons best known to itself, to proceed in retrograde motion between 17 May and 29 June. You may find that you could be going over old ground with siblings, especially if money is at stake. You could be revisiting the scene of earlier passion as well, and if you've moved on and you now have a partner waiting at home you could get yourself into a real tangle.

If you are footloose and fancy free, you are in for a sparkling summer. You won't even have to go very far afield to bump into new and exciting people that push all your romantic buttons. Try socializing locally to make the most of this long period when Venus travels through Gemini.

On 8 August, Venus will be moving into Cancer so it's a rather quiet time where romance is concerned. Your attention is being taken up with what's going on on the home front, and the happiest and most loving time could be spent with your family.

On 7 September, Venus will be moving into Leo, a fire sign like your good self, and you may meet somebody whilst visiting some kind of club, or perhaps taking part in some kind of sport. Either way, you're going to be too busy to think negatively at all. Venus continues in Leo until 4 October when it moves into Virgo. Once more then, it looks as if you're taken over by problems on the working front and you really don't have time or the inclination to think about romance at this moment in time.

On 29 October, Venus moves into Libra, which as you know is your opposite number. This is a romantic and loving period, with you and your partner determined to show each other just how much you mean to each other. If you still haven't found your soul-mate, get into those glad rags and show the world what you've got. You're good company at the best of times, Aries, but now you are on shimmering form. It won't take long before you've found someone to share those cool autumn evenings with. Just the way you like it!

Venus continues in Scorpio from 23 November until 16 December, and once more, then, career matters seem to continue to take over. Luckily, on the 26th, Venus moves into Sagittarius, a fire sign like yourself, and suddenly you remember that you've been squatting at home doing precious little else. Now it is time for you to get out, put on your glad rags and show the rest of us that a 'good time' is really what it's all about; if anyone is going to know about this during this latter part of the month it is going to be you, believe you me.

Health and Diet Year

As an Aries you no doubt know that you have the vitality of an Olympic athlete and the stamina of a plough-horse in its prime. Your energy level seems to be akin to Superman's, however, you use every bit of it, don't you, because you happen to be one of the most active signs of the zodiac. That, of course, can present difficulties because it's all too easy for you to overdo the late nights and keep those heart muscles working over an indecent period.

Your sign rules that head of yours and it's like an over-wound clock that sometimes pushes your body far too long and too hard. The result is, of course, either a case of exhaustion or, in the worst scenario, a heart attack. Not that I wish to alarm you, but prevention is always better than cure, so remember to take it easy from time to time.

In general you hate to be ill and it makes you bad tempered and irritable to be around. This is mainly because you are frightened that you are missing out on something, isn't it? Therefore, the longer you are sick, the more terrible your behaviour! Deep down, you're just like a baby who wants some wonderful new toy to keep you happy, though this is not always available, is it?

Luckily most of the time your health is great, although you have your share of headaches. However, when your temper is aroused germs are not going to hang around for too long, are they?

The chances are that you'll survive to a ripe old age, so don't worry – just try not to drive yourself and everybody else completely crazy. Even when you get to the ripe old age of 100 you'll still be shouting and trying to get other people to give you your own way, and you'll probably succeed too!

Well what about your health during the year ahead? In order to pinpoint potential trouble spots it is a good idea to find out when Mars is in a foul mood because that is when you are most likely to suffer.

During January, Mars is in Aries, which, of course, is your sign. Nevertheless it's not working that well and you need to be alert to burns, scalds and mishaps whilst on the road. A little bit of care is going to take you a long way. During February and March, Mars is in Taurus, which could lead to tonsillitis and other illnesses associated with the throat. However, if you continue to be your usual sensible self, then there is absolutely nothing for you to worry about at all.

During April, Mars will be in Gemini and if the weather is cold and inclement then you need to wrap up in order to protect your lungs. Failure to do so will lead to a great deal of regret, I can tell you. Mars continues in Gemini up until 7 May, when it moves into Cancer and that's the area of your chart devoted to your home. There might be some minor accidents here, so for heaven's sake watch yourself and, of course, your offspring if you have any.

Mars continues in Cancer until 23 June, and so you're really not safe from burns and minor accidents until this date is through. Once Mars gets into Leo, however, there may be

Health and Diet Year

one or two mishaps on the home front, but apart from this you seem to be in rude health.

During July, Mars will be in Leo and for you that is the area of your chart devoted to the good times. If you're taking part in any kind of sport though, you may be prone to grazes, strains and sprains. Possibly you'll say to yourself 'well, I can cope', and you possibly can, but don't overdo it otherwise you could be proved wrong and that would be fatal.

Mars continues in Leo until 9 August when it moves on into Virgo. Strains could occur on the working front and somebody is imposing on your good nature. It might be time to lay down the law and let them know that you're nobody's fool, which, of course, happens to be the truth.

During September, Mars continues in Virgo and you continue to work hard, even though you know secretly that you shouldn't. It'll probably take your partner to stand up for you, or let you know in no uncertain fashion the error of your ways – only then might you listen, but there's no guarantee.

On the 26th, Mars will be entering Libra and that, of course, is the partnership area of your chart so there are likely to be quarrels and disagreements with other people, both at work, in your social life and romantically, and during October, with Mars in Libra, other people will make your life something of a misery. If you haven't already put your foot down, may I suggest that you do so as soon as possible. Somebody is taking advantage and there's no reason why they should – who do they think they are?

Mars continues in Libra until 11 November. After that your relationships begin to improve. However, there may be some kind of stress if you happen to be involved in a legal matter, or you are in the medical profession. It's nice to be kind to your patients but you've got to be kind to yourself too.

During December, Mars continues its sojourn in Scorpio. Therefore, if you can continue to be sensible – and there is 'fat chance' of that – then you should be able to end this particular year hale and hearty. Whether you choose to do so or not is, of course, entirely up to you, but hopefully you will.

Numerology Year

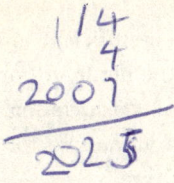

In order to discover the number of any year you are interested in, your 'individual year number', first take your birth date, day and month, and add this to the year you are interested in, be it in the past or in the future. As an example, say you were born on 13 August and the year you are interested in is 2004:

+   13
+   8
   2004
   2025

Then, write down 2 + 0 + 2 + 5 and you will discover this equals 9. This means that your year number is 9. If the number adds up to more than 9, add these two digits together.

You can experiment with this method by taking any year from your past and following this guide to find whether or not numerology works out for you.

The guide is perennial and applicable to all Sun signs: you can look up years for your friends as well as for yourself. Use it to discover general trends ahead, the way you should be approaching a chosen period and how you can make the most of the future.

Individual Year Number 1

General Feel
A time for being more self-sufficient and one when you should be ready to grasp the nettle. All opportunities must be snapped up, after careful consideration. Also an excellent time for laying down the foundations for future success in all areas.

Definition
Because this is the number 1 individual year, you will have the chance to start again in many areas of life. The emphasis will be upon the new; there will be fresh faces in your life, more opportunities and perhaps even new experiences. If you were born on either the 1st, 19th or 28th and were born under the sign of Aries or Leo then this will be an extremely important time. It is crucial during this cycle that you are prepared to go it alone, push back horizons and generally open up your mind. It is time for playing the leader or pioneer wherever necessary too. If you have a hobby which you wish to turn into a business, or maybe you simply wish to introduce other people to your ideas and plans, then do so whilst experiencing this individual cycle. A great period too for laying down plans for long-term future gains. Therefore, make sure you do your homework well and you will reap the rewards at a later date.

Relationships

This is an ideal period for forming new bonds, perhaps business relationships, new friends and new loves too. You will be attracted to those in high positions and with strong personalities. There may also be an emphasis on bonding with people a good deal younger than yourself. If you are already in a long-standing relationship, then it is time to clear away the dead wood between you which may have been causing misunderstandings and unhappiness. Whether in love or business, you will find those who are born under the sign of Aries, Leo or Aquarius far more common in your life, also those born on the following dates: 1st, 4th, 9th, 10th, 13th, 18th, 19th, 22nd and 28th. The most important months for this individual year, when you are likely to meet up with those who have a strong influence on you, are January, May, July and October.

Career

It is likely that you have been wanting to break free and to explore fresh horizons in your career and this is definitely a year for doing so. Because you are in a fighting mood, and because your decision-making qualities as well as your leadership qualities are foremost, it will be an easy matter for you to find assistance as well as to impress other people. Major professional changes are likely and you will also feel more independent within your existing job. Should you want times for making important career moves, then choose Mondays or Tuesdays. These are good days for pushing your luck and presenting your ideas well. Changes connected with your career are going to be more likely during April, May, July and September.

Health

If you have forgotten the name of your doctor or dentist, then this is the year to start regular checkups. A time too when people of a certain age are likely to start wearing glasses. The emphasis seems to be on the eyes. Start a good health regime. This will help you cope with any adverse events that almost assuredly lie ahead. The important months for your own health as well as for loved ones are March, May and August.

Individual Year Number 2

General Feel

You will find it far easier to relate to other people.

Definition

What you will need during this cycle is diplomacy, cooperation and the ability to put yourself in someone else's shoes. Whatever you began last year will now begin to show signs of progress. However, don't expect miracles; changes are going to be slow rather than at the speed of light. Changes will be taking place all around you. It is possible too that you will be considering moving from one area to another, maybe even to another country. There is a lively feel about domesticity and in relationships with the opposite sex too. This is going to be a marvellous year for making things come true and asking for favours. However, on no account should you force yourself and your opinions on other people. A spoonful of honey is going to get you a good deal further than a spoonful of vinegar. If you are born under the sign of Cancer or Taurus, or if your birthday falls on the 2nd, 11th, 20th or 29th, then this year is going to be full of major events.

Relationships

You need to associate with other people far more than is usually the case – perhaps out of necessity. The emphasis is on love, friendship and professional partnerships. The opposite sex will be much more prepared to get involved in your life than is normally the case. This is a year in which your chances of becoming engaged or married are increased, and there is likely to be an increase in your family in the form of a lovely addition and also in the families of your friends and those closest to you. The instinctive and caring side to your personality is going to be strong and very obvious. You will quickly discover that you will be particularly touchy and sensitive to things that other people say. Further, you will find those born under the sign of Cancer, Taurus and Libra entering your life far more than is usually the case. This also applies to those who are born on the 2nd, 6th, 7th, 11th, 15th, 20th, 24th, 25th or 29th of the month.

Romantic and family events are likely to be emphasized during April, June and September.

Career

There is a strong theme of change here, but there is no point in having a panic attack about that because, after all, life is about change. However, in this particular individual year any transformation or upheaval is likely to be of an internal nature, such as at your place of work, rather than external. You may find your company is moving from one area to another, or perhaps there are changes between departments. Quite obviously then, the most important thing for you to do in order to make your life easy is to be adaptable. There is a strong possibility too that you may be given added responsibility. Do not flinch from this, as it will bring in extra reward.

If you are thinking of searching for employment this year, then try to arrange all meetings and negotiations on Monday and Friday. These are good days for asking for favours or rises too. The best months are March, April, June, August and December. All these are important times for change.

Health

This individual cycle emphasizes stomach problems. The important thing for you is to eat sensibly, rather than go on, for example, a crash diet – this could be detrimental to you. If you are female then you would be wise to have a check-up at least once during the year ahead, just to be sure you can continue to enjoy good health. All should be discriminating when dining out. Check cutlery, and take care if food has only been partially cooked. Furthermore, emotional stress could get you down, but only if you allow it. Provided you set aside some periods of relaxation in each day when you can close your eyes and let everything drift away, you will have little to worry about. When it comes to diet, be sure that the emphasis is on nutrition, rather than fighting the flab. Perhaps it would be a good idea to become less weight conscious during this period and let your body find its natural ideal weight on its own. The months of February, April, July and November may show health changes in some way. Common sense is your best guide during this year.

Individual Year Number 3

General Feel

You are going to be at your most creative and imaginative during this time. There is a theme of expansion and growth and you will want to polish up your self-image in order to make a 'big impression'.

Definition

It is a good year for reaching out, for expansion. Social and artistic developments should be interesting as well as profitable, and this will help to promote happiness. There will be a strong urge in you to improve yourself, either your image or your reputation or perhaps your mind. Your popularity soars through the ceiling and this delights you. Involving yourself with something creative brings increased success plus a good deal of satisfaction. However, it is imperative that you keep yourself in a positive mood. This will attract attention and appreciation of all your talents. Projects begun two years ago are likely to be bearing fruit this year. If you are born under the sign of Pisces or Sagittarius, or your birthday falls on the 3rd, 12th, 21st or 30th, then this year is going to be particularly special and successful.

Relationships

There is a happy-go-lucky feel about all your relationships and you are in a flirty, fancy-free mood. Heaven help anyone trying to catch you during the next twelve months: they will need to get their skates on. Relationships are likely to be light-hearted and fun rather than heavy going. It is possible too that you will find yourself with those who are younger than you, particularly those born under the signs of Pisces and Sagittarius, and those whose birth dates add up to 3, 6 or 9. Your individual cycle shows important months for relationships are March, May, August and December.

Career

As I discussed earlier, this individual number is one that suggests branching out and personal growth, so be ready to take on anything new. Not surprisingly, your career prospects look bright and shiny. You are definitely going to be more ambitious and must keep up that positive façade and attract opportunities. Avoid taking obligations too lightly; it is important that you adopt a conscientious approach to all your responsibilities. You may take on a fresh course of learning or look for a new job, and the important days for doing so would be on Thursday and Friday: these are definitely your best days. This is particularly true in the months of February, March, May, July and November: expect expansion in your life and take a chance during these times.

Health

Because you are likely to be out and about painting the town all the colours of the rainbow, it is likely that health problems could come through over-indulgence or perhaps tiredness. However, if you have got to have some health problems, I suppose these are the best ones to experience, because they are under your control. There is also a possibility that you may get a little fraught over work, which may result in some emotional scenes. However, you are sensible enough to realize they should not be taken too seriously. If you are prone to skin allergies, then these too could be giving you problems during this particular year. The best advice you can follow is not to go to extremes that will affect your body or your mind. It is all very well to have fun, but after a while too much of it affects not only your health but also the degree of enjoyment you experience. Take extra care between January and March, and June and October, especially where these are winter months for you.

Individual Year Number 4

General Feel

It is back to basics this year. Do not build on shaky foundations. Get yourself organized and be prepared to work a little harder than you usually do and you will come through without any great difficulty.

Definition

It is imperative that you have a grand plan. Do not simply rush off without considering the consequences and avoid dabbling of any kind. It is likely too that you will be gathering more responsibility and on occasions this could lead you to feeling unappreciated, claustrophobic and perhaps overburdened in some ways. Although it is true to say that this cycle in your individual life tends to bring about a certain amount of limitation, whether this be on the personal, the psychological or the financial side of life, you now have the chance to get yourself together and to build on more solid foundations. Security is definitely your key word at this time. When it comes to any project, job or plan, it is important that you ask the right questions. In other words, do your homework and do go off half-cocked. That would be a disaster. If you are an Aquarius, a Leo or a Gemini or you are born on the 4th, 13th, 22nd or the 31st of any month, this individual year will be extremely important and long remembered.

Relationships

You will find that it is the eccentric, the unusual, the unconventional and the downright odd that will be drawn into your life during this particular cycle. It is also strongly possible that people you have not met for some time may be re-entering your circle and an older person or somebody outside your own social or perhaps religious background will be drawn to you too. When it comes to the romantic side of life, again you are drawn to that which is different from usual. You may even form a relationship with someone who comes from a totally different background, perhaps from far away. Something unusual about them stimulates and excites you. Gemini, Leo and Aquarius are your likely favourites, as well as anyone whose birth number adds up to 1, 4, 5 or 7. Certainly the most exciting months for romance are going to be February, April, July and November. Make sure then that you socialize a lot during this particular time, and be ready for literally anything.

Career
Once more we have the theme of the unusual and different in this area of life. You may be plodding along in the same old rut when suddenly lightning strikes and you find yourself besieged by offers from other people and, in a panic, not quite sure what to do. There may be a period when nothing particular seems to be going on when, to your astonishment, you are given a promotion or some exciting challenge. Literally anything can happen in this particular cycle of your life. The individual year 4 also inclines towards added responsibilities and it is important that you do not off-load them onto other people or cringe in fear. They will eventually pay off and in the meantime you will be gaining in experience and paving the way for greater success in the future. When you want to arrange any kind of meeting, negotiation or perhaps ask for a favour at work, then try to do so on a Monday or a Wednesday for the luckiest results. January, February, April,

October and November are certainly the months when you must play the opportunist and be ready to say yes to anything that comes your way.

Health
The biggest problems that you will have to face this year are caused by stress, so it is important that you attend to your diet and take life as philosophically as possible, as well as being ready to adapt to changing conditions. You are likely to find that people you thought you knew well are acting out of character and this throws you off balance. Take care, too, when visiting the doctor. Remember that you are dealing with a human being and that doctors, like the rest of us, can make mistakes. Unless you are 100 per cent satisfied then go for a second opinion over anything important. Try to be sceptical about yourself because you are going to be a good deal more moody than usual. The times that need special attention are February, May, September and November. If any of these months falls in the winter part of your year, then wrap up well and dose up on vitamin C.

Individual Year Number 5

General Feel
There will be many more opportunities for you to get out and about and travel is certainly going to be playing a large part in your year. Change, too, must be expected and even embraced – after all, it is part of life. You will have more free time and choices, so all in all things look promising.

Definition

It is possible that you tried previously to get something off the launching pad, but for one reason or another it simply didn't happen. Luckily, you now get a chance to renew those old plans and put them into action. You are certainly going to feel that things are changing for the better in all areas. You will be more actively involved with the public and enjoy a certain amount of attention and publicity. You may have failed in the past but this year mistakes will be easier to accept and learn from; you are going to find yourself both physically and mentally more in tune with your environment and with those you care about than ever before. If you are a Gemini or a Virgo or are born on the 5th, 14th or 23rd, then this is going to be a period of major importance for you and you must be ready to take advantage of this.

Relationships

Lucky you! Your sexual magnetism goes through the ceiling and you will be involved in many relationships during the year ahead. You have that extra charisma about you which will be attracting others and you can look forward to being choosy. There will be an inclination to be drawn to those who are considerably younger than yourself. It is likely too that you will find that those born under the signs of Taurus, Gemini, Virgo and Libra as well as those whose birth date adds up to 2, 5 or 6 will play an important part in your year. The months for attracting others in a big way are January, March, June, October and December.

Career

This is considered by all numerologists as being one of the best numbers for self-improvement in all areas, but particularly on the professional front. It will be relatively easy for you to sell your ideas and yourself, as well as to push your skills and expertise under the noses of other people. They will certainly sit up and take notice. Clearly, then, this is a time for you to view the world as your oyster and to get out there and grab your piece of the action. You have increased confidence and should be able to get exactly what you want. Friday and Wednesday are perhaps the best days if looking for a job or going to negotiations or interviews, or, in fact, for generally pushing yourself into the limelight. Watch out for March, May, September, October or December. Something of great importance could pop up at this time. There will certainly be a chance for advancement; whether you take it or not is, of course, entirely up to you.

Health

Getting a good night's rest could be your problem during the year ahead, since that mind of yours is positively buzzing and won't let you rest. Try turning your brain off at bedtime, otherwise you will finish up irritable and exhausted. Try to take things a step at a time without rushing around. Meditation may help you to relax and do more for your physical well-being than anything else. Because this is an extremely active year, you will need to do some careful planning so that you can cope with ease rather than rushing around like a demented mayfly. Furthermore, try to avoid going over the top with alcohol, food, sex, gambling or anything which could be described as 'get rich quick'. During January, April, August and October, watch yourself a bit; you could do with some coddling, particularly if these happen to be winter months for you.

Individual Year Number 6

General Feel

There is likely to be increased responsibility and activity within your domestic life. There will be many occasions when you will be helping loved ones and your sense of duty is going to be strong.

Definition

Activities for the most part are likely to be centered around property, family, loved ones, romance and your home. Your artistic appreciation will be good and you will be drawn to anything that is colourful and beautiful, and possessions that have a strong appeal to your eye or even your ear. Where domesticity is concerned, there is a strong suggestion that you may move out of one home into another. This is an excellent time too for self-education, for branching out, for graduating, for taking on some extra courses – whether simply to improve your appearance or to improve your mind. When it comes to your social life you are inundated with chances to attend events. You are going to be a real social butterfly, flitting from scene to scene and enjoying yourself thoroughly. Try to accept nine out of ten invitations that come your way because they bring with them chances of advancement. If you are born on the 6th, 15th or 24th, or should your birth sign be Taurus, Libra or Cancer, then this year will be long remembered as a very positive one.

Relationships

When it comes to love, sex and romance the individual year 6 is perhaps the most successful. It is a time for being swept off your feet, for becoming engaged or even getting married. On the more negative side, perhaps there is a separation and divorce. However, the latter can be avoided, provided you are prepared to sit down and communicate properly. There is an emphasis too on pregnancy and birth, or changes in existing relationships. Circumstances will be sweeping you along. If you are born under the sign of Taurus, Cancer or Libra, then it is even more likely that this will be a major year for you, as well as for those born on dates adding up to 6, 3 or 2. The most memorable months of your year are going to be February, May, September and November. Grab all opportunities to enjoy yourself and improve your relationships during these periods.

Career

A good year for this side of life too, with the chances of promotion and recognition for past efforts all coming your way. You will be able to improve your position in life even though it is likely that recently you have been disappointed. On the cash front, big rewards will come flooding in mainly because you are prepared to fulfil your obligations and commitments without complaint or protest. Other people will appreciate all the efforts you have put in, so plod along and you will find your efforts will not have been in vain. Perversely, if you are looking for a job or setting up an interview, negotiation or a meeting, or simply want to advertise your talents in some way, then your best days for doing so are Monday, Thursday and Friday. Long-term opportunities are very strong during the months of February, April, August, September and November. These are the key periods for pushing yourself up the ladder of success.

Health

If you are to experience any problems of a physical nature during this year, then they could be tied up with the throat, nose or the tonsils, plus the upper parts of the body. Basically, what you need to stay healthy during this year is plenty of sunlight, moderate exercise, fresh air and changes of scene. Escape to the coast if this is at all possible. The months for being particularly watchful are March, July, September and December. Think twice before doing anything during these times and there is no reason why you shouldn't stay hale and hearty for the whole year.

Individual Year Number 7

General Feel

A year for inner growth and for finding out what really makes you tick and what you need to make you happy. Self-awareness and discovery are all emphasized during the individual year 7.

Definition

You will be provided with the opportunity to place as much emphasis as possible on your personal life and your own well-being. There will be many occasions when you will find yourself analysing your past motives and actions, and giving more attention to your own personal needs, goals and desires. There will also be many occasions when you will want to escape any kind of confusion, muddle or noise; time spent alone will not be wasted. This will give you the chance to meditate and also to examine exactly where you have come to so far, and where you want to go in the future. It is important you make up your mind what you want out of this particular year because once you have done so you will attain those ambitions. Failure to do this could mean you end up chasing your own tail and that is a pure waste of time and energy. You will also discover that secrets about yourself and other people could be surfacing during this year. If you are born under the sign of Pisces or Cancer, or on the 7th, 16th or 25th of the month, then this year will be especially wonderful.

Relationships

It has to be said from the word go that this is not the best year for romantic interest. A strong need for contemplation will mean spending time on your own. Any romance that does develop this year may not live up to your expectations, but, providing you are prepared to take things as they come without jumping to conclusions, then you will enjoy yourself without getting hurt. Decide exactly what it is you have in mind and then go for it. Romantic interests this year are likely to be with people who are born on dates that add up to 2, 4 or 7, or with people born under the sign of Cancer or Pisces. Watch for romantic opportunities during January, April, August and October.

Career

When we pass through this particular individual cycle, two things in life tend to occur: retirement from the limelight, and a general slowing down, perhaps by taking leave of absence or maybe retraining in some way. It is likely too that you will become more aware of your own occupational expertise and skills – you will begin to understand your true purpose in life and will feel much more enlightened. Long-sought-after goals begin to come to life if you have been drifting of late. The best attitude to have throughout this year is an exploratory one when it comes to your work. If you want to set up negotiations, interviews or meetings, arrange them for Mondays or Fridays. In fact, any favours you seek should be tackled on these days. January, March, July, August, October and December are particularly good for self-advancement.

Health

Since, in comparison to previous years, this is a rather quiet time, health problems are likely to be minor. Some will possibly come through irritation or worry and the best thing to do is to attempt to remain meditative and calm. This state of mind will bring positive results. Failure to do so may create unnecessary problems by allowing your imagination to run completely out of control. You need time this year to restore, recuperate and contemplate. Any health changes that do occur are likely to happen in February, June, August and November.

Individual Year Number 8

General Feel

This is going to be a time for success, for making important moves and changes – a time when you may gain power and certainly one when your talents are going to be recognized.

Definition

This individual year gives you the chance to 'think big'; it is a time when you can occupy the limelight and wield power. If you were born on the 8th, 17th or 26th of the month or come under the sign of Capricorn, pay attention to this year and make sure you make the most of it. You should develop greater maturity and discover a true feeling of faith and destiny, both in yourself and in events that occur. This part of the cycle is connected with career, ambition and money, but debts from the past will have to be repaid. For example, an old responsibility or debt that you may have avoided in past years may reappear to haunt you. However, whatever you do with these twelve months, aim high – think big, think success and, above all, be positive.

Relationships

This particular individual year is one that is strongly connected with birth, divorce and marriage – most of the landmarks we experience in life, in fact. Love-wise, those who are more experienced or older than you, or people of power, authority, influence or wealth will be very attractive. This year will be putting you back in touch with those from your past – old friends, comrades, associates, and even romances from long ago crop up once more. You should not experience any great problems romantically this year, especially if you are dealing with Capricorns or Librans, or with those whose date of birth adds up to 8, 6 or 3. The best months for romance to develop are likely to be March, July, September and December.

Career

The individual year 8 is generally believed to be the best one when it comes to bringing in cash. It is also good for asking for a rise or achieving promotion or authority over other people. This is your year for basking in the limelight of success, the result perhaps of your past efforts. Now you will be rewarded. Financial success is all but guaranteed, provided you keep faith with your ambitions and yourself. It is important that you set major goals for yourself and work slowly towards them. You will be surprised how easily they are fulfilled. Conversely, if you are looking for work, then do set up interviews, negotiations and meetings, preferably on

Saturday, Thursday or Friday, which are your luckiest days. Also watch out for chances to do yourself a bit of good during February, June, July, September and November.

Health

You can avoid most health problems, particularly headaches, constipation or liver problems, by avoiding depression and feelings of loneliness. It is important when these descend that you keep yourself busy enough not to dwell on them. When it comes to receiving attention from the medical profession you would be well advised to get a second opinion. Eat wisely, try to keep a positive and enthusiastic outlook on life and all will be well. Periods that need special care are January, May, July and October. Therefore, if these months fall during the winter part of your year, wrap up well and dose yourself with vitamins.

Individual Year Number 9

General Feel

A time for tying up loose ends. Wishes are likely to be fulfilled and matters brought to swift conclusions. Inspiration runs amok. Much travel is likely.

Definition

The number 9 individual year is perhaps the most successful of all. It tends to represent the completion of matters and affairs, whether in work, business or personal affairs. Your ability to let go of habits, people and negative circumstances or situations, that may have been holding you back, is strong. The sympathetic and humane side to your character also surfaces and you learn to give more freely of yourself without expecting anything in return. Any good deeds that you do

Numerology Year

will certainly be well rewarded in terms of satisfaction, and perhaps financially, too. If you are born under the sign of Aries or Scorpio, or on the 9th, 18th or 27th of the month, this is certainly going to be an all-important year.

Relationships

The individual year 9 is a cycle that gives appeal as well as influence. Because of this, you will be getting emotionally tied up with members of the opposite sex who may be outside your usual cultural or ethnic group. The reason for this is that this particular number relates to humanity and of course this tends to quash ignorance, pride and bigotry. You also discover that Aries, Leo and Scorpio people are going to be much more evident in your domestic affairs, as well as those whose birth dates add up to 9, 3 or 1. The important months for relationships are February, June, August and November. These will be extremely hectic and eventful from a romantic viewpoint and there are times when you could be swept off your feet.

Career

This is a year which will help to make many of your dreams and ambitions come true. Furthermore, it is an excellent time for success if you are involved in marketing your skills, talents and expertise more widely. You may be thinking of expanding abroad for example and, if so, this is certainly a good idea. You will find that harmony and cooperation with your fellow workers are easier than before and this will help your dreams and ambitions. The best days for you if you want to line up meetings or negotiations are going to be Tuesdays and Thursdays and this also applies if you are looking for employment or want a special day for doing something of an ambitious nature. Employment or business changes could also feature during January, May, June, August and October.

Health

The only physical problems you may have during this particular year will be because of accidents, so be careful. Try, too, to avoid unnecessary tension and arguments with other people. Take extra care when you are on the roads: no drinking and driving, for example. You will only have problems if you play your own worst enemy. Be extra careful when in the kitchen or bathroom: sharp instruments that you find in these areas can lead to cuts, unless you take care.

Your Sun Sign Partner

Aries with Aries

This relationship can have tremendous possibilities if you both decide that you don't have to be boss at the same time. At first, you'll woo each other with more aggressive enthusiasm than is seen at a political meeting. However, when he starts acting dictatorial, she starts getting pugnacious because she's not being treated like she's the President – these two hot tempers can easily melt steel.

Both are passionate, energetic, with new ideas, and romantic in a flighty kind of way. Together, you can stay up all night shouting, waving your hands in the air, and planning how to design a new tennis ball that bounces seven feet higher. However, when 5.00 a.m. comes, and he settles back happily to announce that it was all his idea, she is not above setting fire to the couch he's sitting on.

Since a bad case of the Me complex pervades both consciences, they sometimes have a hard time hearing each other. You both love to confess how great you are, but sometimes forget to mention that the other is really pretty good too. However, it's not unlikely that the Aries would compliment his (or her) lover by commenting 'you have to be fantastic, extraordinary and wonderful if you have me'.

The gentle art of humility is not one of your fortes. As a matter of fact, you probably don't even know what 'humility' means, since it's one of those words that is much too subtle for your dictionary.

Between yourselves, however, there can be much sympathy, kindness, understanding and compassion, and between your bodies a tremendous amount of passion and sensuality. He will love the way her mind moves. She will love the way he seems to wield his power single-handedly.

Initially, you will gravitate to each other like two warships meeting during peacetime. After that, the cannons just keep shouting off. And so do your mouths. This relationship is bound to be both highly tempestuous and trying on the nerves. But you'll both find that it's worth it. Only Aries can stand this insane excitement and then stick around to create more.

Aries Woman

Aries woman with Taurus man

He won't exactly appreciate the way you point when you want something. Likewise, you won't like the way he refuses to move when you point.

You are bossy and used to wrapping men around your little finger and squeezing hard. Although he would be willing to climb Mount Everest for some woman who would ask him nicely, he doesn't at all appreciate the pushy touch.

You operate from the principle of the faster the better, while he can't see why anything is worth doing if he has to kill himself. You are impatience personified; he wouldn't mind waiting for the sun to turn green. You are the classic super achiever who can never get enough power. He is the first to sit back and settle for what he has.

Sexually, this is a good match; however, he won't like it if you have other men too. Basically, you don't believe in Mr Right, and therefore are always open to the casual affair. You are adventurous, while he loathes risk taking. You are committed only to the moment; he is ready to sell his soul to satisfy his future needs.

Your energy will excite him, but his energy won't exactly send you soaring. You want to be challenged, but he wants to be made to feel secure. You have a hunger to be at the top, whereas he gets satisfaction from staying somewhere in the middle.

Together, you both seem to be moving in different directions, but only you seem to be going somewhere, and it's probably out of his life, since his stability makes you anxiety-ridden. However, in the long run he is far better off with a woman who doesn't even know the time, but who does know how to walk without running.

Aries woman with Gemini man

You are so powerful and controlling that if he wants to play your game, it's got to be by his rules.

Your healthy sexuality will be an encouragement for him to keep his mouth shut. His insane sense of humour will make you laugh at yourself for the first time in your life. He's enamoured of your energy while you are galvanised by his enthusiasm. He loves your courage, while you love his sharp tongue. You are so fast that you truly intrigue him, while he is so changeable that you don't have time to lose interest.

Initially, this attraction is exciting. However, if he makes a commitment that he doesn't carry through, you'll get him, but good. You have a temper that will shake him out of his jocular senses, and, in addition, you will probably have more strength than he does. If he tries to play games with you, he'll just get a cold seat on your doorstep, because you really don't have the time. There are too many men waiting for your attentions, and the world is waiting for your leadership.

Therefore, if he behaves capriciously, you'll forget his first name as he is left somewhere in mid-sentence. The only way to win you back is to appeal to your passion. It's worth it, though, because you are one exciting female who is never going to be forgotten.

Aries woman with Cancer man

He is a truly lovable person, but his love is not meant for you. Your fiery outbursts will send him into a sullen withdrawal – and his sudden withdrawals will send you into more fiery outbursts. Together, you are so different that you seem to be coming from two countries that have never known the other was even on the map.

Emotionally, he is super-sensitive, though he hates to show it. And you have a way of hurting his feelings even by the way you ask a polite question. His feeble attempts to camouflage his vulnerability make you chew your nails. His moods make you more impatient. And his apparent passivity makes you stamp your feet just to break the silence.

Basically, he would rather spend a quiet evening home cooking while you would like to be at a party until dawn. You like to think you are conquering the world, but he likes to comfortably occupy a very secure part of it. He works hard for his future comforts, and you work hard just to work. He is interested in having a family, while the closest you want to come to children is to knowing him. You create continual excitement; he seeks security at all cost.

Just to be dramatic, you might tell him that you're leaving him, and calmly he will remind you to take your cold tablets and credit cards. If you want a life full of drama with Mr Cancer, then you'd better go to a film. Otherwise, you should pick someone else to raise your pulse rate.

Aries woman with Leo man

If he gets in your way, you'll stand on his feet and ask him what he's doing there. He's always had a yen for aggressive women, and you are a dynamo. Your energy levels are amazing, and at times he has to jog just to keep up.

Because you love a challenge, he will inflame you with his flirtation. After you decide that you want him, you'll take over and move in so fast he'll feel passive by comparison. You are direct, and always take the shortest route between two points. His sense of dignity might dissolve because of your candour. Yet, at the same time it'll mean that you don't take up his time with trivia.

You are headstrong, independent and ambitious, and dedicated to doing what you please. If he doesn't hold you back your achievements will exalt him. Since your anger is like a blowtorch, he should try to be his supportive self rather than a bully who criticizes. Deep in your heart you know you were born to be the best, and you won't listen for a second when he berates your boastfulness. You live your life to enable the world to come to the same conclusion, and if he hints that you're not perfect, you'll shout that he's mumbling.

Your love of life will rejuvenate his brain cells, and your passion will ignite his senses. Together, you are passion personified, and when you sit side by side, the world seems to shrink away. When your egos are controlled, this attraction is magical, but when they collide, the fights that result would make the sphinx blink. But if he can be less ego-oriented, you will be his.

Aries woman with Virgo man

He'll remind you to comb your hair as you dash madly out of the door for an important appointment, and nag you when you throw your clothes all over the floor. He'll point out the trail of unfinished projects, and when you're late, lecture you on the necessity of discipline.

His approach to life is so cool and logical, at times you'll wonder if he has something missing. On the other hand, he will wonder at your need for constant hysteria, and may lose sleep worrying about your smoking and drinking. The basic difference here is that you take everything to extreme, while he keeps to the safe middle ground.

He is cautious while you throw caution to the wind. He is frugal while you can be capricious with money. He has a personality that is reserved, and you have one that can't be held back. He likes quiet moments, whereas you seek the excitement of crowded places.

Needless to say, you two aren't exactly compatible. However, you both could learn a great deal from this relationship – if you are willing to listen.

Aries woman with Libra man

His indecisiveness will drive you to just short of sheer insanity, while you'll make him nervous and depressed as you injure his self-esteem. Any way you look at it, you are not an easy woman for him to contend with. You are blunt and outspoken, while he likes his women to be subtle and genteel. Your hot temper will terrify him, and you are so commanding that he will feel sick whenever he tries to say no.

At first he was drawn to you – like a lamb scampering towards the butcher. However, after a few shaky scenes he will come to decide you are worse than his mother, and even the fact that you may be famous would hold no appeal for him.

You want a man who will announce to the gods that he has never been so in love, but even if Mr Libra tries this, the chances are that the original feelings won't last long. It is far more likely that you will torment him just to say something, and what he will say is that he really doesn't know what to say. While you are waiting impatiently for him to scream that he would die for you, he will no doubt mutter instead that he has no idea what he feels.

Undoubtedly, the most romantic statement he'll make, after the initial novelty wears off, is that he doesn't want you, although you are a very nice person. Ms Aries and Mr Libra are made for that blistering romance that lasts as long as the holiday does. What happens after that time is a truly sobering experience that neither of you will want to face sober. So it might be best to just drink up and travel fast in different directions.

Aries woman with Scorpio man
This combination is passion personified, but it is one that involves a primitive kind of power struggle, and your egos will clash hard enough to bruise you both.

You'll get miffed if he talks about himself rather than musing about what a mysterious woman you are. And you'll get mildly outraged when he doesn't seem to be ready with those compliments. You'll try to boss him around, and if he doesn't do as you say, you'll step on his foot. In turn, he'll snarl and throw out a few viciously sarcastic comments – however, you won't even be listening.

You charge around like a warrior, and although he admires your strength, he resents your lack of subtlety. He likes to be the aggressor, but somehow you always beat him to the punch. He respects your drive, your worldly accomplishments, your vitality and stamina. And in turn, you want him, but you're not sure that you respect him. The question is: do you even notice him unless he trips over you? In the long run, only the bruises will tell.

Aries woman with Sagittarius man

While he is definitely a delightful adventurer, you may consider him too capricious to cope with.

Sure he is charming, exciting and has a sense of humour that arrests your total attention. However, at the same time, he makes you feel so insecure that you may wish you'd never met him.

You have to be first, and with this man you always feel that you're merely one of his many interests – women, projects, crazy schemes. While you love the freedom to engage in impromptu flirtation, no way do you appreciate your man doing the same. Eventually he will bring on bouts of jealousy that will send you to bed – with someone else.

Although he may take you sky-diving, ballooning and shooting the rapids, he will also tread on your ego so badly that he may need either a plaster-cast or time away from you in which to recuperate.

You like his outspokenness, but hate the way he speaks the truth. You know you've gained 5 lbs during the past week, but there really must be something wrong with his eyes if he can see it. This man will remove your sense of being in control, because your coercive tactics just leave him cold. Therefore, you will have to put your ego away, and be your most charming and patient. You always relish a little competition, but what we have here is a basic battle of needs and wishes. And any way you look at it, if you want to gain something, you will have to lose something else.

Aries woman with Capricorn man

He'll worry that you work so hard that you'll end up catching a bizarre disease. You'll angrily reply that he's being over cautious. Deep down, Mr Capricorn is a good soul who means well, but on the outside, you may at times find him a bit gloomy – he could have written the original disaster movie, it's true. And at times you may consider him to be something of a sourpuss. However, if you disregard his pessimism and concentrate on his sense of responsibility, you might find a man worth meeting, knowing and perhaps loving.

If he makes a commitment, you will remain uppermost in his mind, and he will never try to evade what he feels he has to do. However, he is controlling and chauvinistic, and he embraces a double standard that you may have to break down before he can get any further. He has advice to offer on every subject, which you might find somewhat irritating, since you're not used to listening to unsolicited opinion.

He will find you exciting, stimulating and provocative, but at the same time a little crazy. He'll admire you for your drive, determination and ambition, but he'll question the way you go about getting what you want.

If both of you can relinquish your individual needs to supervise and control, and put your energies instead into trying to understand each other, this relationship could take you any place that you might want to try to go. It's worth the battles that will come about as a result of the effort. Just keep in mind that it's not the fighting that matters but the resolutions that really count.

Aries woman with Aquarius man

He is the ultimate challenge, and you'll hate to admit that he's got you. You think he has a beautiful mind, while he thinks you have a beautiful body. You feel that you can't get enough of him, but unfortunately he's not caught in the same vortex of emotion. He likes women, men, dogs, cats, etc. He's not a snob – he'll speak to anybody. Naturally this bothers you since you want to overwhelm him to the point where he'll beg to follow you anywhere. However, in this instance you'll be the one who is doing the following, and, without planning it, he's the leader.

Because his basic attitude is that he has nothing to lose, and because yours is that you stand to lose more than a lot, he holds the key to your heart. When you lose your temper, he'll walk away; when you threaten to leave him, he'll calmly say 'go ahead'. When you try to make him jealous, he'll mention that maybe you'd be better off with someone else. When you try coercing him, he'll tune out while he gives his attention to another woman. The basic difference here is that he is detached from his ego while you are attached to yours.

Aries woman with Pisces man

Your temper will give him nightmares, but what you do in his daydreams is quite another matter. He is destined to fall flat on his face in love, but you won't want to hear or see it.

He is too subjective for your sensitivities, and has a way of making you feel like you're working in a clinic for the emotionally disturbed. He tries your patience, never gets to the point, and drives you insane with his moods. You need a man who is strong enough to push you around after you've stepped on his feet. However, Mr Pisces will just stand there and let you.

At the same time, you need a lot of love and approval, and Mr Pisces can truly drown you in devotion. However, when his sentimentality starts to ooze, and you suddenly feel more suffocated than aroused, he just knows he's nearing the beginning of the end.

He sees you as a sadomasochistic kind of challenge. You see him as a noose around your neck that keeps getting tighter. At the end, through his tears, he'll wish you the worst. But you'll wish him the best, as you rush out of his life forever, possibly screaming.

Aries Man

Aries man with Taurus woman
You're pushy, while she's placid. You're impatient, but she just waits for change. You're flighty, and she never gets off the ground. But the very worst is that you're so bossy that sometimes she wants to bribe you to shut up.

You see yourself as very exciting, and you'll tell her about it. But what you won't tell her is that you have a temper that could make her swallow her bubblegum.

Unless she has a lot of Aries in her horoscope, this relationship is better off left as an encounter. For a Taurus woman to lose her heart to an Aries man is like an orphan in a storm watching a wealthy family celebrate Christmas.

Aries man with Gemini woman

She admires the way you connect your mind to your body, while you respect the clever way she utilizes her mind. This is like a first-sight infatuation where you take each other places – everywhere from the tennis courts to the bedroom. She'll get your total attention when she gives little killer jabs to your ego. You get her total attention when you don't call when you said you would. She tells herself she couldn't care less, but watch that tension wrenching at her stomach.

If one of you can break through the verbal barrier and even mumble in your sleep 'I love you', the chances are that you might both end up happily married. However, that's not to say that you won't test each other the entire way to the church.

Aries man with Cancer woman

She'll fall in love with your dynamic enthusiasm, but undoubtedly will get hurt by your lack of emotional understanding. She needs more nurturing than you know how to give and has more insecurities than you can handle.

On the other hand, she is that woman you can count on and the person who will hold your hand and listen to your problems. She will support you with sincerity that you might find irresistible. She will love you with a loyalty that inspires your respect and she will give you the kind of understanding that you could easily find addictive.

Aries man with Leo woman

This is nothing less than love at first sight when you dash aggressively to her side to retrieve the diary she has deliberately dropped. You're quick to pick up her cue. And complimentary – especially when she lets her eyes drift. You adore the challenge of winning her, and her many flirtations give you many challenges. The problem is that your flirtations give her indigestion. She can't imagine why you would ever consider glancing at a bland-looking blonde slinking by, when she is the grand lady of glamour. If you knew enough, you would be blinded. After all, when you're with her, it's theatre, not a free-ring circus.

Between you there's much warmth, passion and mutual admiration. You're one of the few men who can get away with telling her what to do. You know it, and this excites you even more. You're enthralled by her energy and enthusiasm. And you respect her independence and ambition. Her warmth and support spur you on to far-reaching goals.

Aries man with Virgo woman

You'll teach her how to do exercises and preach to her the virtues of keeping fit. You'll have her mesmerized when she watches you eat steak for breakfast and play eight hours of tennis in the blistering sun. Yes, you get her attention alright, and she admires your energy, respects your ambition and feels a little wondrous at your constant enthusiasm. But despite your vitality, she has a hard time trusting you, especially when you call her at midnight, or 4.00 a.m., to ask her out and then stand her up because something else catches your attention.

You need immediate gratification, while she is willing to wait a while for something meaningful. You're looking for a challenge of a lifetime, while she would just like a little love. You want to get drunk as you look into her eyes, while she simply wants to see some warmth in yours.

Aries man with Libra woman

She'll make your life a beautiful place to live in and you will give her the romantic excitement she so needs. At a candle-light dinner, she'll drown you in tones of Mozart, as well as in her favourite vintage Burgundy. You'll feel like a sultan as you sit in the lap of loving luxury. In return you will sweep her off her feet and leave her feeling shaky but blissful. Sexually you will take her by storm and give her strings of sleepless nights that she'll come to count on. Your unbridled passion will take her places she's never been to before. However, it's where she feels she's going that she worries about.

Aries man with Scorpio woman

You'll sweep her off her feet and carry her over the threshold. And for once, her mind will stop calculating whether she's going in the right direction. However, since you're both coming from such opposite places, this passion is short-lived and in any prolonged involvement she'll start to think of you as both selfish and silly.

You're all energy, passion, vitality and promises. You'd rather run than walk, but often the direction is in circles.

Aries man with Sagittarius woman

She will consider your ego problems silly, and you will consider her behaviour flighty. She has a lot of energy, but in the long run never seems to have very much to show for it. However, she can ruin your self-image on the tennis court and can outdo you in stamina on a bike ride. Once you overcome your basic self-centredness, the chemistry here can catalyse a very intense kind of love.

Both of you are freedom loving, friendly and optimistic. Her good-natured support will help you to get your ideas off the ground. Your active sense of competition will spur her to do something with her life and not just talk about it.

Aries man with Capricorn woman

On the surface she is cool and steady, while on all levels you are a crazed madman who means well. Therefore, you'll be enthralled at the way she carves her way to greatness and in the process cuts out all the hysteria.

She will be a little overwhelmed as you come dashing into her life, almost knocking her door off its hinges along the way. She'll think you're nice, but maybe from another planet when you move about in her living room like a Mexican jumping bean and start doing push-ups in the middle of a conversation. You will excite her with the way you get enthusiastic over the flavour of ice cream, and you will make yourself unforgettable in your repertoire of bedroom activities. However, if you want her to really warm to you, you have to exercise a little patience. This Capricorn wants a man who is dependable, unlike you; she doesn't seek a circus where the action in the main ring never ceases.

Aries man with Aquarius woman

She awes you with her humanitarian idealism, and you overpower her with your lists of achievements. She is the kind of woman you love to talk to, and you are the kind of man with whom she likes to listen; beyond this, the basic difference is that you are a taker and she is a giver. You are absorbed by self-interest while she has an interest in every person who crosses her path. With you, the chances are that she will end up giving far more than she's getting. And Aquarius is so good-natured that she has a bad habit of sacrificing her own inclinations to other people's strong desires. You can be demanding, jealous and possessive, although you'll fully expect the freedom to do as you please. Yes, in this relationship there are going to be plenty of temper tantrums, that is until one of you decides to exit stage right.

Aries man with Pisces woman

For her, it is almost love at first sight, whether or not she wants to show it. But that's just the sexual starters. After the first few nights, you could still be in the running for a total ravishment of her mind and body. However, after she witnesses how selfish you can be in the daytime, with the sun shining in your eyes, then it's quite another matter if the love continues.

She is still searching for that knight on a silly white horse to come and whisk her away. Superficially, you'll fulfil her fantasies, but underneath, not only will you not understand her, you won't even have the patience to try.

She has a way of getting her feelings hurt at the most inconvenient moments, and you have a way of treading on them without either realizing it or wanting to be made aware of doing so.

Your Child of the Zodiac

Your Aries child doesn't get any less accident-prone as he or she grows older. If you're wise you will instil in your child a healthy respect for sharp objects and fire, but you will have to resign yourself to a never-ending stream of minor cuts, bruises and scratches, especially on the face and the head. The vulnerability to infection is invariably present where Aries is concerned, and should your child's temperature shoot up within a matter of seconds, you can be fairly certain that some law of hygiene has been broken.

A tendency to headaches is also likely, especially should your child be under any kind of stress. Mental problems and earaches are a common occurrence, and nightmares are a problem with a Ram child, often traceable to some kind of friction at school. It is important that you communicate and discover what is worrying your child. The Aries infant does have a tendency to keep worries and problems to him or herself. Gentle persuasion will help to unlock the mental door the child may attempt to keep shut.

Young Rams display many war-like traits! Although on occasions this can lead to physical violence, the Aries child will generally prefer to fight verbally. Conflict stimulates the Ram and arguments among friends will be a rule rather than exception. A bloody nose and a bruised lip can usually be chased back to the best friend and not an enemy. Such a child is independent, original and sports loving. He or she will usually be found taking part in school activities – the usual result of being so popular. Loneliness in an Aries child is a rare thing indeed.

Clever parents realize the importance of entertaining children's friends. If the child is accustomed to bringing home loud and noisy friends now, it will be natural to do likewise when older. If you are fiercely house-proud and don't like the thought of being invaded, set aside a couple of rooms (if possible) for the use of the Aries child and his followers, buy some earplugs and prepare for the mess once the party has departed. Better this than a child who sneaks off to heaven knows where later on.

An Aries child doesn't like to sit still for any length of time. Sports, especially running and gymnastics, appeal to both sexes. If you are a devious parent you will reward any good efforts by buying books on a much-loved sport. In this way you'll be killing two birds with one stone!

Drama also appeals to the egotistical Ram and this should be encouraged. The Aries imagination isn't strong, but such an activity will stimulate it. Nevertheless, they can easily be persuaded that there are really fairies at the bottom of the garden! However, reality is much more important to the Aries rather than fantasy. You are also likely to discover that your child is attracted to speed. Skating, scooters, skating-boards and so on, will all appeal but remember that accident-prone head and make sure he or she wears a helmet.

Of course, we all worry about our children – it's only natural. This one, however, needs a little bit of extra care because of its reckless behaviour. Nevertheless, who can resist an Aries child? Nobody of course!

Monthly and Daily Guides

JANUARY

The Sun this month will be drifting along in the earthy sign of Capricorn up until the 20th, and this is the area of your chart, of course, devoted to work and professional matters; as usual you could go to extremes from time to time. Remember that life is about 'balance', and you need to spend just as much time with your family as you do with your boss, if at all possible.

On the 21st, the Sun will be moving into Aquarius and that's the area of your chart devoted to friends, team effort, acquaintances and matters related to clubs on a social level. It looks as if your social life is going to be extremely hectic and, of course, you'll enjoy every moment of this.

Mercury, wouldn't you know, is in retrograde action in the sign of Sagittarius at the beginning of January, but fortunately only during the first week. After these few days, it finally begins to see sense, so do postpone signing important contracts, or taking long-distance travels no matter what the reason may be until after the 5th, if at all possible.

Venus will be in Aquarius until the 14th, throwing a rosy glow over relationships with friends and acquaintances.

However, on the 15th, it moves into Pisces and that's a rather secretive area of your chart. This will mean that your instincts will be extremely good, and you may be making plans for the future. But try to wait before impulsively rushing ahead.

Mars will be in Aries, your sign, all month and you need to take care here because the impulsive side to your character will be uppermost and you could make mistakes that might lead to little injuries, such as cuts, burns, etc. Be especially watchful in the kitchen and make sure that children are well out of your way when you are doing your cordon bleu meals for friends.

Furthermore, if you have any Aries friends you're likely to be getting together with them far more than is usually the case and enjoying the experience. January is likely to be an extremely lively month, so make sure that you enjoy it as best you can.

Lastly, the pattern made by the stars during January seems to suggest – wouldn't you know it – that you'll be starting many projects, relationships and situations but without properly considering the consequences. Try to make sure that you do think things through a bit, and all should be well.

1 THURSDAY There's a certain rift between several planets and this will give you your fair share of decision making. You don't mind hard work but you do need to play as well. Boredom will make you do something extreme. But giving up those structures you've created, especially when you're proving how determined you can be, is something you might regret later. Over the next few days you'll find a way to enjoy yourself and live in a more liberated fashion.

2 FRIDAY Today the stars remind you to consider why you don't trust someone. You may be unmoved by the high regard

Monthly and Daily Guides: January

they are showing you, but that person is grinding away behind the scenes for your benefit. Remember – they're on your side. You'll be thankful for their input very soon.

3 SATURDAY Don't let someone special harbour resentments now you're sure of your feelings. The planets bring a long-awaited turning point. It's true that you're over critical, but now you can be direct, open and genuine.

4 SUNDAY Crystallizing those dreams and schemes is paying off, but the planets' influence certainly is slowing down the pace. Stick to your intentions. However well meaning others are, they don't have your ability to see all the options. Tell them you'll do it your way or not at all – you have more integrity than you think.

5 MONDAY You're feeling freer to say and do as you please. Your mind is working faster than usual, and you're getting more support, instead of blank looks. Your more ambitious plans will soon be taken seriously, and a bonus will come sooner than you think.

6 TUESDAY Today you'll be rather impulsive, acting first and thinking later – so what's new? There will be an Aries tendency to take on many things, or relationships, without thinking things through satisfactorily. Luckily though, now that you're aware of the fact, you should be in a position to do something constructive about it.

7 WEDNESDAY Today is the day of the Full Moon and it occurs in the watery sign of Cancer, that's the area of your chart devoted to home and family, which means that there could be some discord. Perhaps not everyone in the family is going to agree with plans you've made for the future. However, if you turn on the charm how can they possibly resist?

8 THURSDAY The stars are giving you a chance to say what's on the tip of your tongue. Deep down, you know what others' response will be. Remember you won't be able to go back on your word once spoken, so it's time to have faith in your feelings – they really are important.

9 FRIDAY Others insist they are right and you're wrong. The planets today are making various people highly principled. Their thoughts are interesting, but you can't be expected to bow down to unorthodox methods unless you've created them. Avoid arguments by agreeing to differ.

10 SATURDAY Damaging though others are, look again at a more radical definite goal. The more flexible you can be, the more likely you are to reach a mutual turning point in a relationship. The way forward, disruptive or not, is likely to be extremely liberating.

11 SUNDAY Your personal planets are urging you to think long and hard and seriously about your goals. It's time to explore new possibilities, especially as you're not prepared to commit yourself to someone else's fanciful ideas. You're besieged by all those things you would most like to escape from, but soon you'll be making a clean break, never fear.

12 MONDAY A rising sense of restlessness is due to the planets. All of those repressed issues are emerging, such as what you really want to do with your time and how to balance what

Monthly and Daily Guides: January

brings joy with what is routine. It's unsettling, but at least you have a chance to sort out your needs, just be rational.

13 TUESDAY Friends can't get the gist of your argument, but don't waste time trying to explain. You can push too many psychological buttons without meaning to at this moment in time; however, this does give you enthusiasm and helps you to act positively. It might take a while before others realize you are right though, as they have their own issues to resolve.

14 WEDNESDAY You can't take on more than you want to at this time. Others don't have your ability to take massive leaps forward and the planets are giving you a kind of efficiency that others will envy. For peace of mind, don't think you must sit back with other people. Be spontaneous and you'll get results.

15 THURSDAY Cooperation is needed with loved ones. They could feel you have neglected them when you've had other things to think about. Treat others affectionately and this will be a more than pleasant surprise for them – it will also be one for you too.

16 FRIDAY Invest in yourself for a change, instead of always being generous with your time. While working matters are running smoothly it seems a shame not to take advantage of this to attend to your own needs. Although you would prefer to be organizing everyone else, sometimes it's more rewarding to coordinate personal affairs that are your life-blood too.

17 SATURDAY It isn't difficult to commit yourself to a lucrative proposition, but it does sting a bit having to admit that someone else came up with the idea first. The planets are giving you a chance to start a new dialogue, which will prove who has the most to offer and the best staying power. You know you'll be the winner.

18 SUNDAY You might come across as charm itself when discussing your latest undertaking, thanks to the influence of the stars. It seems your down-to-earth enthusiasm is rubbing off on the right people. It might be more appropriate, however, to hold back on negotiations for a few days until others are less hungry for a slice of your popularity.

19 MONDAY Now you've finally decided what you want, you're going to get it. It is essential, though, to take into consideration the needs of your family or loved ones. Remember, not everyone has the determination to see things through to the bitter end. Make allowances for someone's inconsistency and restlessness – you'll be pleasantly amazed at the outcome.

20 TUESDAY A mystery needs clearing up. Although someone is assuming they can't sort it out themselves, it might be more profitable if you unravel the threads first. You know you're in a position of power, even though it feels a little uncomfortable. Better to take the initiative rather than miss out on an opportunity for progress.

21 WEDNESDAY Today is the day of the New Moon so it's a good time for putting the finishing touches to work, and a relationship too, but it's not an ideal time for pushing ahead with ambitious plans – bear this in mind.

22 THURSDAY You are willing to make a commitment but a connection may turn out to be a complete success or a complete wash-out. You're feeling pressured into making firm promises. Whether others can reach a compromise is irrelevant. You have to cement an association or bring it to a swift conclusion.

23 FRIDAY You wish to widen your options and give yourself a chance to change your lifestyle, but not everyone has your motivation and adventurous spirit. Just this once tell someone special that you're leaving them out of the equation, in order to work on your possibilities. During the next couple of weeks or so you will discover that keeping promises is worth the commitment, especially when you have a chance to leap forward to where you least expect to be.

24 SATURDAY Persuasion is needed if you're going to market yourself and you've got all the necessary qualities. If someone doesn't have the same level of belief in you, it's time to prove how seriously dedicated you are to your success. You don't have to be ruthless, just use your integrity. It's what other people love about you.

25 SUNDAY An unresolved meeting doesn't mean you are at a standstill. You have every right to be impatient, especially as others aren't keeping their side of the bargain. Don't push them for answers. Remind them you need to see some sign of life. Then they might begin to realize there is major value behind your minor flaps.

26 MONDAY If someone appears hard-headed you have little choice but to shrug your shoulders. Your own sense of dignity cannot be penetrated, and it won't hurt to be impervious to their dogmatism. You're beginning to wonder if others are as supportive as they pretend. It would be wise to find out.

27 TUESDAY You are feeling innovative but it would be wiser to ride with the general consensus of opinion. That means navigating a financial matter with care. The planets are reminding you that sometimes it's better to hold back and wait for others to take your ideas seriously – that way you'll be certain you don't get yourself into a mess.

28 WEDNESDAY It is possible that today you seem aloof and unapproachable to work colleagues. The time has therefore come for you to be less defensive. You understand their wants and needs and by placing these centre stage you will be making new friends and associates. Also, you will derive a great deal of benefit from considering a career change.

29 THURSDAY Marvellous thoughts are crossing your mind and you want to tell everyone about them because of the planets' set-up today. Although you're fascinating and inspired for your own good, you are also a little tactless. Remember that when sharing ideas you can be a little indiscreet from time to time.

30 FRIDAY Vitality is something you are feeling in abundance, and it seems that someone special has noticed your surge of energy. Devote your attention to sorting out a rather silly difference of opinion. You're finding it relatively easy to reach simple conclusions, and cultivating more harmony will also give you a better sense of your own needs.

31 SATURDAY Don't strike out too rashly if someone seems to be holding back. It's fair to say that your ambitions contradict their more conservative approach, but perhaps you'll let them express their thoughts, especially as what you want to change in your working life could be a crucial issue. Explore it sensibly.

FEBRUARY

The Sun this month will be drifting through that eccentric sign of Aquarius, which is the area of your chart devoted to friends, contacts, club activities and team effort, all of which are well starred; if you want to make any important moves in any of these sides to life then push ahead.

On the 19th, the Sun will be moving into Pisces, and the area of your chart devoted to instincts, intuition and what is going on behind the scenes. There's a likelihood, too, that you'll be able to sort out a 'wrangle' that has been going on for quite some time; now you and your partner see sense and life seems to be a good deal easier.

Mercury will be in Capricorn during the first week and that's the area of your chart devoted to your ambitions and your work. You may have to travel for the sake of your job, or perhaps meet new people – either way things look promising.

Venus is in Pisces up until the 8th. Oh dear, it looks as if you're being a little bit dishonest where relationships are concerned. Perhaps you've got a strong sexual attraction for somebody on the working front, but if you make a move I'm afraid you're going to be found out and that special relationship of yours could come to a grinding halt. Take care.

Mars will be in your own sign of Aries for the first couple of days. You've got abundant energy and are determined to get your own way, but try to use a little bit of tact. Mars will be moving into Taurus on the 3rd – the financial area of your chart. Oh dear, it looks as if you're going to really rob your own bank account and spend, spend, spend. Perhaps you have met a new admirer, but there's no need to try and 'buy' them; they're already besotted with you anyway – try to keep this in mind.

The pattern made by the stars during February suggests that you're more dependent on other people: perhaps you've got some ambitious plans but you're not quite sure whether you're going in the right direction, therefore, you are airing your views to others in the hopes that they will back your plans. The chances are they probably will. Push ahead without fear.

1 SUNDAY Admitting that you have feelings is always nerve-racking. But it's time to put all of those sentiments into words for someone special. Try as you might, you feel the planets are urging you to be romantic. It's worth being a little spontaneous now you're in such an exuberant mood. Sharing your thoughts is the best tonic.

2 MONDAY It's incredible that you have the urge to sort out your joint resources or finances and you have a very shrewd sense of what's wrong. The planets are making you push home a very serious issue. If others don't feel like discussing the matter then you have little choice but to organize everything yourself. That way you can sleep soundly.

3 TUESDAY Today Mars will be moving into Taurus, which is the area of your chart devoted to money. Mars tends to be one of the 'greedy pigs' of the zodiac, which means that you could be spending without due thought. If you rush along headlong into an extravagant spending spree I'm afraid that partner of yours is going to be displeased and arguments could ensue for perhaps a couple of days – be sensible.

4 WEDNESDAY For someone so light-hearted you're suddenly in a rather sober mood. It's not that you want to be surrounded by long faces but you are generally fed up with superficial comments. The danger is that others might think you're trying to get one up on them. Grin bravely but don't give anything away until you are in a more candid frame of mind.

5 THURSDAY Domestic or family affairs are becoming distinctly more agreeable. And there's almost a feeling that you can talk about anything and not have to justify yourself. Of course, that doesn't mean you can get away with critical comments. What it does suggest is that you can get your heart off a very tenuous subject. Take the chance while you're so spirited.

6 FRIDAY Today is the day of the Full Moon and it occurs in the fiery sign of Leo. That's the area of your chart devoted to the good times and romance, so it looks as if there is about to be the beginning of a beautiful friendship. Whatever transpires will work to your liking, so be bold and never fear.

7 SATURDAY This is a day for reflection and one when you need to understand that it is necessary to re-educate yourself into reacting to every situation and problem in a more constructive fashion. Try putting your principles first, rather than your popularity with other people. In this way you will soon learn how to deal with long-standing financial or material problems.

8 SUNDAY Mercury is now well entrenched in the airy sign of Aquarius – an excellent time then for team effort, for taking small gambles, both financially or simply for the 'hell of it' and high spirits, and if you happen to be single, you will be attracting others to you in a big way.

9 MONDAY Today Venus will be moving into your sign so you're looking good, feeling great and are ready to socialize and make love around the clock. If you already have a partner the next few days are going to be extremely hectic; if you don't have anyone in view this is likely to change over the next couple of days or so – have fun.

10 TUESDAY When your mind is set on achieving something new and lucrative, there is little that can stop you. It seems that your recent negotiations are proving successful. Just take care you don't shout too loud, or too long, in someone's ear. They have to take it all at a different pace. Now is the time for patience, attention and discretion.

11 WEDNESDAY What you have had to put on hold is now beginning to gel and it's time to take action. In the nicest possible way the planets are giving you the chance to negotiate freely, so don't pass up your opportunity to put your more controversial views across. You might sound arrogant but there's nothing like a spot of provocation to get you noticed.

12 THURSDAY Your intuition is telling you to make certain commitments but your mind is still weighing up the pros and cons. Although you are acting with more ambition and drive than you have for a long time, there's a feeling that you might end up gaining nothing. Don't let your fears and doubts rock a very lucrative boat. It's time to set sail.

13 FRIDAY Trust your instincts regarding a friendship. Sometimes you imagine all kinds of negative things about others for no good reason. Doubting their belief in you will make you less confident. The planets are making others highly cooperative, so don't think it's a myth that you are in demand – you really are, so enjoy yourself.

14 SATURDAY Don't take offence just because someone is getting more attention than you are. The planets are making you feel angry beneath the surface. A gnawing resentment will mean you'll lose out on a very satisfying contract. Irritated though you are, transform your edginess into enthusiasm. That way you won't bear a grudge for long.

15 SUNDAY Someone has a bright idea, thanks to the stars. Just for once let them make the decision and lead the way. You've already planted a few seeds about how you want things to develop, so now you can sit back and watch the plot unfold exactly as you intended. Don't let on it was your idea in the first place – it's more fun.

16 MONDAY Even if someone else doesn't seem enthusiastic about your viewpoint, it won't be difficult to shrug and smile. You know matters concerning your private life are certainly in question, but you're not prepared to back down now. Maintain that harmonious atmosphere and let others do their own thinking. They'll soon realize you have a very good point.

17 TUESDAY Composed as you are, there are a few outstanding obligations that won't go away. If you attend to them immediately, you'll have time to enjoy the company of some special people. Try being true to yourself for a short while and you'll realize how profitable your honesty is. You are about to discover that others see you in a very worthwhile light.

18 WEDNESDAY It's best to keep busy and if you remain optimistic you'll achieve much. You've got a million things you want to discuss but never the time to say them. Be patient, you don't want to wear yourself out trying to find the right time – the moment will come soon enough. Those who doubt you are going to have a real shock when you reveal your success.

19 THURSDAY Today is the day when the Sun will be moving into Pisces. As this is the secretive area to your chart, you will find yourself making a great number of plans. However, it wouldn't be a good idea to act just yet. Be patient.

20 FRIDAY Today is the day of the New Moon and it occurs in the watery sign of Pisces. This a very secretive area of your chart, and you may feel unusually introverted. You may discover that by keeping your thoughts to yourself, your grey cells are stimulated to come up with some very clever ideas, especially where work's concerned.

21 SATURDAY Family and friends are asserting their needs at the moment, so it would be tactful to keep your opinions to yourself. There is much to be said to a few in-depth conversations, but only if you do so without rebuking others. Accept they have a very different attitude to certain arrangements. Be careful not to tip the balance too much in your own favour.

Monthly and Daily Guides: February

22 SUNDAY Foolishly someone is still trying to wind you up and push your emotional buttons. But you have the feeling at the back of your mind that you're getting bored with the game. After all, you always said you weren't contradicting them. Generally you have been calm and relaxed about the whole thing, but now it is time to show your true colours, and be a true Aries too.

23 MONDAY As much as you want an exciting life, it seems others aren't giving you the chance and your enthusiastic plans and schemes are still being ignored. So it might be worth sharing your thoughts with someone special just to stir up their interest. You never know where it might lead – hopefully to a more trusting relationship, with a million sparks of passion too!

24 TUESDAY Whatever your romantic intentions are, keep it nice and simple when expressing them. If you're feeling shy about revealing your thoughts, don't forget others are expecting you to open up. It's not really the words you say that matter, but the feeling behind them. You've got nothing to lose right now if you take the plunge.

25 WEDNESDAY Avoid putting your foot in it when others make a great deal of fuss about nothing. They may, of course, be right to complain but you can hardly believe they are causing such a scene. Assertive as you are, you won't help anyone in the long run if you go off at a tangent sorting out their problems. Give them time to come around. You'll be thankful for the change of air.

26 THURSDAY Imposing your will over others could cause a temporary conflict of opinion. You're not looking for a verbal fight, but among friends you might suddenly have the justification to do just that, especially as they're equally responsible for playing mind games. So answer back, however vulnerable you are.

27 FRIDAY You may not have been honest enough with yourself, particularly when it comes to how much you're willing to give up on behalf of someone else. Rather than being torn between submissively cooperating and avoiding the issue altogether, use your judgement to establish exactly what you will and will not do. You'll both feel better for it.

28 SATURDAY Emotionally you might fear what lurks within, and you have no reason to delve deeper than is necessary. But isn't it the feeling that if you don't face up to what you dread most in yourself, you might lose some very valuable insight? There's a considerable power to your frivolous façade so don't be afraid to live it out.

29 SUNDAY Certain aspects of your private life are taking up your time, and trying to avoid the demands made on you won't be easy. You would prefer to be more radical about certain issues, so keeping your mind open is probably the best course of action. It's hardly likely to cause any on-going mutual conflicts, especially if you can make the effort to listen.

MARCH

The Sun this month is glistening away through the water sign of Pisces, which is, of course, a secretive area of your chart. Your instincts are firing on all cylinders and should really be listened to. Don't let others interfere by telling you that you are wrong, because you most certainly are not.

On the 20th, the Sun moves into your sign so you begin what is known as your 'solar year'. Certainly you're far more confident than is usually the case, so heaven help other people. You're also at your most ambitious and won't think twice before treading on the toes of workmates, but do remember this probably won't make you very popular, so be a little thoughtful.

Mercury is in the sign of Pisces up until the 11th, so you may have a lot of paperwork which needs attending to. Just for once you're in the mood to do it, so that you'll have time to enjoy yourself later on in the month when Mercury moves on into your own sign.

Venus is in Taurus from the 6th of the month, and this is the area of your chart devoted to finances. If you happen to work in anything creative you'll certainly be putting on a good show and others are going to be madly impressed. Furthermore if you need any advice, and you have a Taurus in your life, this is the person to go to.

Mars continues in Taurus until 20 March. Hang on to your possessions when in crowds because you could very well lose something due to somebody else's light fingers. Quarrels about money may crop up too and somebody's got to see sense so it might as well be you.

Luckily, on the 21st Mars moves into Gemini, and that certainly livens up your mind as well as your body. If you're tackling anything demanding in any area others will appreciate all your good efforts. You can't really go wrong at this moment in time, Aries, but don't think too much – just enough to make sure you're on the right track and you certainly will be.

The pattern made by the stars during March indicates that just for once you're thinking more about your home life rather than always striving to achieve great things at work. You can be quite sure that your loved ones are going to appreciate this fact.

1 MONDAY Express your desires and intentions while you're feeling so formidable. The planets are affecting the part of your chart where someone will love you as you are, so don't think you have to be anything other than yourself, especially as you'll also be on the same wavelength. That means that you can both take pleasure in the same very moving experiences.

2 TUESDAY If someone is playing hard to get, or simply being awkward, it's not your fault. Be prepared to boost their confidence a little and they could turn towards you, rather than away. While you're wrapped up in your dreams, they are trying to be realistic. Of course, visions for the future matter, but so does the present.

3 WEDNESDAY Over the next few days you need to realize that one intimate relationship is improving. It's not that you're unduly worried, but you are aware there are certain issues that need resolving. Trust in your open approach to life. Your optimistic side is certainly about to be given a boost, and with that comes a better understanding of why others admire your qualities. You will feel so much better for the knowledge.

4 THURSDAY Charming though someone special is, take care that you don't become complacent. The more you express your desires and needs the more likely it is that your principles won't suffer. You owe it to yourself to acknowledge your differences; that way love could be a greater security than you imagined. It just takes a conscious effort on both sides.

Monthly and Daily Guides: March

5 FRIDAY You undoubtedly want to spend time organizing others while they are so compliant, but don't assume that their laid back attitude can be taken for gratitude. Make a gallant effort to notice their needs and desires too. You don't like hostility, so work on your own creative ideas, otherwise you'll run the risk of robbing other people of theirs.

6 SATURDAY Today is the day of the Full Moon and it occurs in the earthy sign of Virgo which is the area of your chart devoted to your workmates and to routine. It's quite possible you'll be making new contacts where ambitions are concerned, and this will lead to a more hectic social life over the next few days or so.

7 SUNDAY Saturn finally resumes direct movement on this day, so from hereon in, though you may still be carrying a good deal of responsibility, it will be a great deal easier for you to cope with. Furthermore, others are willing to lend a hand, so don't be too proud.

8 MONDAY You're not sure that someone isn't taking advantage of you, but think about it carefully. Perhaps you are denying the possibility of your fear of loneliness. But what do you hope to gain from their association? Enjoy their company – it means you're wanted – but don't judge a book by its cover. There's more to this than meets the eye.

9 TUESDAY Express your most eloquent ideas to people who are willing to back you up. The stars are giving you the chance to finalize any plans you made a few days back, but you still need to know one particular individual is on your side. Genuine praise and support is one thing, vague compliments could mean that they just don't know what else to say.

10 WEDNESDAY Are you afraid to be special? If you can't honour your individuality, then no-one is going to recognize your unique qualities. Luckily today you have some time to yourself to think things through. But don't betray chances of success for the sake of living up to other people's high expectations.

11 THURSDAY Money issues are highlighted by the stars but that doesn't mean you have to get yourself wound up with the ins and outs of all the details. For once allow yourself the privilege of detaching yourself from someone else's assumptions about what you should and shouldn't do. Instead, enjoy a little financial flutter. It will do you the world of good.

12 FRIDAY Today Mercury will be moving into your own sign, which makes you much more adaptable, and there's a possible longing for adventure too. You could satisfy this, of course, by booking a holiday for the summer. Failure to do so could mean that you'll be chasing rainbows, which really isn't a very good idea, I think you'll agree.

13 SATURDAY Your heightened sense of optimism is inducing you to think carefully about your long-term goals. You're living your life the way you want to regardless of what other people say. When it comes to approaching other people the direct way is the best one.

14 SUNDAY It's almost as if you are suddenly seeing your future ambitions in a new light. And that can't be bad when you've had so many recent setbacks. Now, you're on the verge of a very different set of objectives, and it pays to be shrewd and well informed. What you are about to discover is that your style of handling matters is how you achieve results. Do it your way, and you won't regret it.

15 MONDAY All your efforts to establish a more intense connection with someone are going to be worthwhile. Whatever anyone says, you have the courage and the energy to leap through more than one blazing hoop. Even if you rile a few people in the process you are at least making it clear that you won't give up on yourself for their benefit.

16 TUESDAY Recent changes in your working situation have been welcomed, but now you are running around in circles trying to keep up with yourself. There's nothing like fast pace action to give you the feeling of making headway – just take care that you don't give up on a more amusing diversion at the expense of exaggerated ambition.

17 WEDNESDAY You're being rewarded for your input even though there's nothing much to show for it on the surface. Then again, what goes on behind the scenes is often more complex and subtle than that which is out on view. Trust in the stage management rather than the players. Your success depends largely on how your whole performance is put together.

18 THURSDAY You may still want freedom for all, but it seems that you are the last person to give it. Containing yourself to certain patterns of behaviour won't enable you to be liberal with yourself. Unconditional love is possible if it's a two-way thing, but think carefully about whether your ideals are as boundless as you make out.

19 FRIDAY Living by your wits alone doesn't seem to be enough. You're gradually realizing that the moments when you know how to act are the ones that come from an inner place. Intuition is giving you a profound feeling about the rights and wrongs in one relationship – more pertinently, imbalance and love aren't mutually exclusive.

20 SATURDAY It's a busy day in the stars and this is because the Sun will be moving into your sign so you begin what is known as your solar year, giving you extra confidence and oomph to get out into the world and make your mark. Furthermore, the New Moon is beginning to show itself too, also in your sign, so really this is a 48-hour period in which you must do everything important should you want success and, of course, you most certainly do.

21 SUNDAY You will suddenly discover that someone you have known for a considerable length of time has been holding a torch for you, and this relationship could last for a number of weeks. It will bring a great deal of happiness, but make sure you are honest with the person concerned because they are most certainly being honest with you.

22 MONDAY Mars has moved into Gemini now, so you'll become much more adaptable and easy-going over the next couple of weeks or so. If you have any members of this sign in your circle, they are the people who will provide you with the most fun and games, so get out into the big wide world and make it see things from your point of view.

23 TUESDAY This will be an extremely rewarding day and it's particularly good if you're involved with anything connected with legal affairs or foreigners. Therefore, push hard in these sides to life but, of course, use a certain amount of charm too.

24 WEDNESDAY There's always something very inspiring about a challenge, particularly when it concerns your ambition. You're beginning to realize that you can make all kinds of waves when you want to. You have your own reasons for coercing others, but extend your thinking to more liberal ideas and give up all that brainstorming. Others will love you for it.

25 THURSDAY Certain people around you have very hungry egos. This means it's easier to take a back seat and let them get on with it. Your personal values are beginning to revolve around a new set of precedents so assert yourself a little bit more than usual. If you make an effort it won't stop a clash of temperaments, but you'll achieve much more than you would by sitting back.

26 FRIDAY The stars are certainly making you far more interesting when you put your message across, but certain onlookers could make you think one thing and then say another. If you're fighting for a personal cause, speak your own heart. However, avoid appearing rebellious. It won't do you any favours when others are so conservative.

27 SATURDAY It is understandable that you want to put your life on a more steady basis. However, you seem to be using a bulldozer to open a gate. What you must first do is to try to relax and not be quite so tough on yourself. You can be sure that loved ones, friends and relatives like you for what you are and not for what use you can be to them.

28 SUNDAY You don't usually have a problem letting off emotional steam, especially when others are being awkward or unresponsive, but some doubt about your own assertiveness is shown. Face up to the fact that even you can sometimes glamorize a situation that doesn't exist – and that's exactly what you're doing right now.

29 MONDAY These are challenging times and to cap it all you're now dreaming about achieving something new. Don't just leave it to your imagination. You have the courage and strength to put your ideas into practice as long as you don't let twinges of doubt get in your way. Although you're understandably nervous, persuade yourself to act now.

30 TUESDAY The emotional undercurrents between you and an intimate friend aren't exactly stable. True you are always ready to adapt to moods and whims, but sometimes even you have to draw the line between your own needs and feeling obligated to theirs. You are much better off when things are out in the open. Be a diplomat – that's what you're going to be good at right now.

31 WEDNESDAY It would be silly to assume every aspect of your life can be tied up simultaneously. After all, impulsive action will only make it feel as if it's never going to happen. But it will. Making justifications to others for changing your private affairs won't exactly be easy, but take one step at a time and everyone will be in agreement.

APRIL

The Sun will be drifting along in your own sign in April, well up until the 19th anyway, and so this is the part of the year known as your solar year because it contains your birthday. The Sun will flood you with confidence and there's nothing you cannot achieve once you put your mind to it. However, do make sure you look at the fiddly little details, because these often mean you come a cropper.

On the 20th, the Sun will be moving into Taurus – the financial area to your life. All of a sudden you realize that you haven't got as much in the bank as you had thought and you become quite miserly for a couple of days, or even a couple of weeks. Never mind; I'm sure that partner of yours is used to your strange behaviour, so all should be well.

Mercury, of course, is always a changeable planet and it will be coasting along in the sign of Taurus, shilly-shallying and going backwards and forwards at this particular time. Never mind, Mercury always has been mischievous and I don't think anything's going to change at this moment in time.

Venus will be in Taurus during the first few days, which will be useful if you need to chase anyone for money – you may even have a bit of luck! On the 4th, Venus moves into Gemini, the area of your chart devoted to short trips, special acquaintances and creativity. If you happen to be fancy free, you may crash into a rather exciting proposition on the romantic front, so make sure that you are alert to this possibility, won't you?

Mars will be in Gemini all month. It is, of course, your ruling planet and because of this you temporarily take on some of the characteristics of this sign, becoming much more adaptable, chatty and communicative. If you have any

Geminis in your circle be diplomatic, they may have some problems and they won't thank you for telling them exactly what to do – they know what they're doing themselves, thank you very much.

The pattern made by the planets is a rather scattered one and this could suggest that going in any one direction could be somewhat difficult. However, if it is important that you do stay on track you'll have to muster all of your willpower in order to do so, because if you keep veering from left to right and back again I'm afraid you won't get very far at all.

1 THURSDAY Certain ideas are occurring to you about how to make your life more stimulating. In fact, you're feeling quite excited about a current change in a relationship. Although it's for the better, someone else can't seem to get their head around all the pros and cons involved. Speak up while you're feeling so insightful. You have precious little to lose.

2 FRIDAY Today Mercury will be moving from fiery Aries into the sign of Taurus and that's the area of your chart devoted to money, possessions and high finance. Many of you will be signing a contract in connection with one of these areas, and if you so you've certainly picked the ideal time for doing that. However, do be a little bit careful from the 6th onwards, because after this date Mercury goes into retrograde movement and that could make life somewhat complicated.

3 SATURDAY Rather than making a fuss on principle about a working matter, why not let the situation speak for itself? You know you're right, and if others can't face up to the facts then they'll just have to grin and bear it. You're feeling confident enough to persuade anyone around to your way of thinking.

The minor problem is their complacency, but it won't last for very long.

4 SUNDAY Today Venus is moving into Gemini and the area of your chart devoted to short journeys, which should be extremely enjoyable. It looks then as if you are entering a period when there's a great deal of to-ing and fro-ing, new faces, general excitement and perhaps even new romance. It seems that you have a great deal to look forward to, which is very nice.

5 MONDAY Today is the day of the Full Moon in your opposite number, Libra. Any signs of weakness in others might just be because they fear your disapproval. And you're the last person to be judgemental at the moment. You know exactly what it's like to feel sentimental but dislike displays of emotion. If you've someone special in your life it would be a good ideal to tell them exactly how you are feeling and that will bring you both closer to one another.

6 TUESDAY Today is the day when Mercury moves into retrograde movement. Therefore, while this planet is in such a mood, it would not be a good idea to sign any important documents; procrastinate maybe for ten days or so before jumping into the fray because otherwise you could seriously regret it.

7 WEDNESDAY Objectivity counts, particularly regarding working matters, but it's not like you to be so inconsistent. Frankly, others aren't making your life any easier by changing the rules. A sudden revelation that you're right will bring you to your senses. Then others will realize you need space to do things your way, just for once. This will work to your advantage.

8 THURSDAY Don't cut yourself off from your feelings just because everything is getting too emotional. There's been an awful lot of dialogue, but it's mostly been hot air. Now is the time to establish what someone really means. You're usually able to negotiate the most complex of situations but even you have to admit you still have moments you would prefer to avoid.

9 FRIDAY This could be a difficult day if you're travelling, so double check your plans and don't make any changes. Romantically your judgement is totally off and you're in danger of deceiving yourself. Why not spend this day being closer to those people in your life who really count. You might as well because precious little else is happening, and it would be nice to end this day on a lovey-dovey note, wouldn't it?

10 SATURDAY You have so many thoughts crowded into your mind at this moment, that it might be difficult for you to concentrate on any one thing for any length of time. Even so, you really must try hard today to get to grips with cash responsibilities or duties which should have been dealt with a long time ago. Now as one of the fiery signs of zodiac you might secretly believe that minor matters are beneath you, but I'm afraid even you need to get down to the humdrum, boring bits of life from time to time and this is a good day for doing just that.

11 SUNDAY The stars seem to be pulling you in several directions today; they strongly urge you to pay what is owing and then move on to something, or maybe even someone, new. You know you have to come down to earth sometime, just like the rest of us, so it might be a good idea not to put it off any longer. It's time for getting your duties out of the way, boring as they may seem.

12 MONDAY It's true that people you deal with every day will be at their most awkward, but so will you. There's no point in trying to explain your motives because they simply won't be listening. Make sure you avoid situations that make you angry or stressed.

13 TUESDAY Generally speaking you have a great deal of confidence, but for some reason you are hesitating about approaching other people; come on, Aries, you're known for your bravery so best hoof forward. You can be quite sure that anything you discuss with others will be well received, but perhaps you're fretting about damaging your fragile ego.

14 WEDNESDAY The stars today combine to give you a remarkable chance to make important decisions which are needed in your life. Do go where your instincts take you and don't think twice about waving goodbye to people or things that, for too long, have been holding you back. If your work is connected with foreign affairs, teaching, or the need for good ideas then you can expect to 'make your mark' on this day.

15 THURSDAY There may be some news that you have been waiting for connected with an official matter, or with people who have control or say in your financial life, such as your insurance broker or your bank manager. All these seem to be emphasized by the stars, but in a good positive way. So if there are any problems, now is the day for ironing them out, when the stars are very much on your side.

16 FRIDAY Today is the day when many of you will become sexually or romantically involved with a person who works perhaps in connection with foreigners, or to do with travel. It looks as if you're about to begin a learning phase. However, any worries you have in connection with somebody who contributes to the household on a financial level will begin to melt away and you can heave a sigh of relief.

17 SATURDAY Those of you who have been looking for backing for one of your grandiose schemes have probably been running into a brick wall. Contracts can also be a source of loss and travel will be have been complicated of late. Luckily this state of affairs begins to evaporate over the next few days and you will lose that feeling of walking through treacle.

18 SUNDAY The word 'change' is emblazoned across your chart now and providing you refuse to give in to fears about matters you aren't well acquainted with, you'll benefit in ways you had never expected. The planets are encouraging you to reach out into life and be prepared to grab some of the opportunities with your eager little paws – and why not?

19 MONDAY Today is the day of the New Moon and, guess what, it falls in your sign. This could be a red letter day, so make sure you look good before you leave home and be ready to grab any opportunity for enjoyment, success or anything that needs that extra touch of luck.

20 TUESDAY Today is the day when the Sun will be moving through your own sign. You could hardly go wrong, unless you really try, but don't even think about it, just be ready to grab all opportunities that come your way.

Monthly and Daily Guides: April

21 WEDNESDAY This is quite a good day if your work is at all creative and you should be able to use your intuitions and your imagination as they are firing on all cylinders. Naturally, it's important that you do your homework but, having done so, you must take your courage in your hands and allow other people to see those 'little gems' that you have been able to come up with.

22 THURSDAY Today is the time when you will ask yourself some difficult questions, but the answers you are hoping for are closer to hand than you think. The stars help to shift your perspective and see things from a new and dramatic angle – you may even decide to uproot and start again in a completely different setting.

23 FRIDAY The stars make you finally realize that a physical move in life is perhaps not enough: what you really need now is a whole new way of living, or philosophy if you like. The stars are leading you to withdraw and become introspective. There's nothing wrong with this as long as you don't take it too far, because, let's face it Aries, you are a creature of the sunshine and by hiding away you're going against the grain. Even so, a short period of seclusion could be extremely beneficial.

24 SATURDAY Today is the time when you should take advantage of anything that comes completely out of the blue. Those closest to you, both within the family and in your friendship circle, are fiercely energetic and highly sexed too – how nice. This evening you may feel like putting your feet up and probably your partner will join you, one way or the other.

♈

25 SUNDAY This is a good day where you are feeling a little bit detached, unorthodox and humane. This means you'll be doing little kindnesses to other people for a change – don't think that they won't notice and be grateful.

26 MONDAY There's a certain amount of luck and growth over all of your relationships, both professional as well as personal. If you've been emotionally involved with the same person for quite some time and that relationship has become rather stale and uninteresting, this is the time when you should make some changes. Do so before you decide to throw in a towel because you could regret it at a later date.

27 TUESDAY Today the stars could be transforming you. However, if you decide a gigantic clear out is needed then make sure you don't throw away something that is important. Remember the saying about throwing the baby away with the bath water because once you have jettisoned something, or someone, out of your life it may be difficult to get them back again.

28 WEDNESDAY Today there's a certain amount of tension or disruption. Even your long-made plans may disappear as if by magic due to changing circumstances and, really, the only thing you can do is to stay alert as well as you possibly can from morning to night. It's a time when things won't turn out the way you expected.

29 THURSDAY There's a good chance that you're going to be rather restless and impatient today, and those who know you well won't be the least bit surprised if you take off somewhere at the drop of a hat. If you haven't cleared up things with work colleagues, bosses or partners first, then you must expect a few obstacles to be placed in your path.

30 FRIDAY If you decide to take a risk concerning your personal and financial security, now is the right time for doing so, because you are at your most original – almost bordering on genius – and because of this, ideally, you must really ignore what other people are saying and listen to your own small voice. It knows the answers while other people are still arguing about the questions.

MAY

The Sun this month will be digging its way through the earthy sign of Taurus up until the 20th and that's the area of your chart devoted to money. Now, normally, you are only too happy to empty your bank account on behalf of children, loved ones and other people, but from hereon in you're playing everything rather close to your chest, which can be no bad thing, because just for once you may actually be able to save, well, for a while anyway.

On the 21st, the Sun will be moving into Gemini and that's the area of your chart devoted to communication with other people, over both long and short distances. Furthermore, you may be bumping into new friends and acquaintances whilst you're going about your everyday business and, one way and another, this seems to be rather an enjoyable and busy time.

Mercury continues in your sign Aries until the 15th, so you're much more animated, innovative and ready to take on board changes, some major and some simply minor. All in all, it's a stimulating period which you're sure to enjoy.

Venus will be in Gemini all month, and the area of your chart devoted to communication and friendship. If you're at all artistic, be it professionally or as a gifted amateur, the results you achieve will do a great deal to please you. However, Venus starts slipping backwards into retrograde movement on the 17th, and matters related to emotions and affairs of the heart could be somewhat complex. Try not to be stubborn; take on board other people's ideas and all should be well.

Your ruling planet, Mars, will also be in Gemini until the 6th, which means that there could be some friction or misunderstandings where brothers and sisters are concerned. Siblings invariably fall out from time to time, but somebody's got to be all grown up – see what you can do.

Mars will be moving into Cancer on the 7th where it stays for the remainder of the month. There could be some squabbles and tension on the home front, or perhaps in connection with property. Try to make sure that you are the grown up here. If you can do that then others will follow suit and peace will be maintained. It's up to you.

The pattern made by the stars is a rather scattered one. Oh dear, this seems to suggest that concentration is suffering; there's loads of good ideas for the majority of the time but you must make absolutely certain that you finish what you start, whether this be a project, romance or family matters. Failure to do so will lead to inefficiency and something you'll be kicking yourself for many months to come. Of course, whether you decide to take this advice is entirely up to you.

1 SATURDAY If you have any major investments or purchases to make right now, you should hesitate no longer. Soon you will discover that money is inclined to flow out at a considerably faster rate than it's flowing in, so spend where it's absolutely necessary but, at all times, keep a weather eye on the future and any repercussions which may occur from your actions at the moment.

2 SUNDAY You must, of course, know that you are born under a rather rash and impulsive sign. This can be either a blessing or a curse, depending on how well you're managing your finances, and whether or not you have limited your spending to essentials only.

3 MONDAY On no account should you allow yourself to be led into 'risk taking' because if you do, you'll finish up poorer. Not only that, but you will incur the anger and disappointment of those who mean the most to you. This can be an enjoyable time but is absolutely nothing to do with the amount of money you spend, only the company you keep.

4 TUESDAY Today is the day of the Full Moon and it occurs in the watery sign of Scorpio, which is the area of your chart devoted to big business, insurance matters and shared resources. It would be a good idea to hang on to your precious little trinkets if you're thinking of visiting places which are overcrowded; failure to do so could mean that you'll lose something and you'll kick yourself for quite some time.

5 WEDNESDAY Those who are closest to you are going to be in the mood for making changes – you had better behave yourself just in case you are one of them. You may not altogether agree with their suggestions but they are determined to push on despite warnings or advice that may come from you, so you may as well sit back and be ready to pick up the pieces if you really believe they're heading for a fall.

6 THURSDAY It may be necessary for you to travel on this particular day. Therefore, you'd be wise to double-check all of your arrangements – visas, passports, tickets and other documents – because if something can go wrong you can be quite sure that it will. It would be a good idea to remain courteous and helpful where foreigners are concerned, because they are likely to be unduly sensitive.

7 FRIDAY It looks as if there's a minor new cycle occurring in one of your relationships, or perhaps somebody new and exciting will enter your life. Certainly that special someone is full of warmth and generosity and will honestly be going out of their way to do the right thing in order to please you. Make sure you return their kindness, and a happy day is sure to be enjoyed by all.

8 SATURDAY This is a time when you can certainly gain from the ideas and suggestions of other people – always assuming, of course, that you can pocket your fierce pride. New people will be entering your life, so if you're already in a serious romance complications may crop up, not that you'll mind; this seems to pique your curiosity as well as providing you with an ego boost and what Aries can possibly resist that?

9 SUNDAY There seems to be much going on around you at this time and your first impulse may be to keep yourself hidden until all the fuss dies down, however, you should enter the fray and sort things out. After all, no other sign is better qualified to create order out of chaos, and by the time the stars are in a very different aspect peace and serenity should have been restored.

Monthly and Daily Guides: May

10 MONDAY The stars today suggest that a calculated risk could very well pay off, but this must be well thought out. The chances to enjoy yourself this evening seem to come in multiples: sports, romance and party-going are all well starred. Mind you, it's not surprising you're so popular because, let's face it Aries, you're one of the most charming people under the zodiac. Well, you can hardly say this yourself, so I'm doing it for you.

11 TUESDAY You're in a strange mood on this particular day, perhaps because you've precious little to do, so why not think of some imaginative ways for fattening up your bank account – and, my goodness, doesn't it need it? What's more, you'll be prepared to face any problems or complications that exist in any area of life and you'll be sorting out everything with common sense for a change, as well as facing up to the act that you simply can't carry on spending money at the current rate.

12 WEDNESDAY Today you'll be tempted to take on competitors and rivals to show them exactly who is boss, but why waste time on people plainly too dumb to learn from their mistakes? Besides, the stars are stirring up your friendship circle so you won't be short of chances to enjoy yourself. This is a wonderful time for visiting clubs, taking part in team sport and indulging in casual flirtations – mind you, the latter may not be a good idea if you have a partner in tow.

13 THURSDAY You may not be able to forgive, but it is in your interest to forget any insults or sleights which have been hurled in your direction. Put the past behind you and concentrate on your happiness. It's time you stopped fretting about what others are doing and start to pay more attention to your own needs and desires. The stars suggest that you may decide to 'hole up' this evening in order to think through life's major decisions.

14 FRIDAY You need to snap up any opportunity which seems to be right under your nose, so do so soon, otherwise you may be swept along in a tidal wave of change that you are powerless to influence, or even control. The stars suggest there is serious money to be made from the unusual, or even an outrageous idea – so what are you waiting for? Remember you have the confidence to dare and now is the time to prove it.

15 SATURDAY Something could enrich you one way or another today. This, of course, could be through experience but it may also be connected with something to do with money. The thing to do is to listen to propositions both at work and at home and be absolutely certain that you don't let an opportunity or a chance pass you by. If you do you'll be kicking yourself from here to next week.

16 SUNDAY Today Mercury is making ready to move into Taurus and that's the area of your chart devoted to money, of course. It is therefore quite likely that that which is owed to you will come rolling in. Although you may be tempted to 'splurge' this wouldn't be a good idea. Instead lock your illgotten gains away in the bank; you never know, you might need it some rainy day when it definitely pours down.

17 MONDAY It appears that you have finally learnt that a soft approach to other people's life can pay far more than being aggressive and manipulative. Because of this there seems to be

Monthly and Daily Guides: May

a 'getting together' with other people and in doing so you'll both be forgetting and forgiving past differences, sweeping them under the carpet and preparing to start all over again, which can be no bad thing. A minor celebration would be a good idea this evening.

18 TUESDAY You can certainly expect some change and movement in your circle of friends, acquaintances and contacts today; this is because your emotions are easily moved at the moment. Perhaps, where you were once madly attracted to someone, interest now is beginning to waver. Conversely, where there was once little interest, curiosity could be beginning to increase. Certainly then, this is not going to be a day in which you can expect to be bored – quite the reverse. You're going to be on your toes from morning till night and revelling in all of the action.

19 WEDNESDAY Today is the day of the New Moon and it occurs in the earthy sign of Taurus, the area of your chart devoted to cash matters. This is good news, because there's a possibility of somebody putting a good idea or project in your direction. Think twice before you turn it down – if you do, you'll be incensed by your stupidity at a later date.

20 THURSDAY If you need a time for facing up to bureaucrats, officials, the taxman or your bank manager, make an appointment and do so over the next couple of days, because they simply won't be able to resist your charm. They will also respect your honesty, and the plans you have made for the future. So get out your thinking cap, because although it would be nice to ignore these areas to life, unfortunately they have a way of cropping up when we least expect them.

21 FRIDAY Today is the day when the Sun will be moving into Gemini and if you've any friends born under this sign these are the people to go to if you need any kind of help or assistance. Yes, I know you're fiercely independent and you can cope on your own, thank you very much, but we all need a sounding board from time to time, and this happens to be one of those days.

22 SATURDAY The stars are hinting that you may be sorely tempted to try and get away with something but, Aries, you're such an open personality that you are bound to get caught if you give in to this temptation. This is a splendid time for meeting new people and acquaintances, though you may not be able to keep their friendship for very long. It is more a case of ships passing in the night rather than dropping anchor in your harbour.

23 SUNDAY It looks as if a friend or acquaintance has decided to sit you down and talk some financial common sense into you, which, of course, won't get them very far, because nobody can tell you how to run your life, not unless they are prepared to lay down their life in the process. Mind you, if this is an emotional contact and they are simply reaching out, then you are more likely to listen and let them have their say.

24 MONDAY Today you can certainly gain from partnership affairs and anything creative. However, if you're given an inch where money is concerned, Aries, you'll take a yard – which roughly means that although money may be coming in, you'll be heading straight for the glitzy shops eager to spend your pennies on something completely frivolous. Now, if you have any kind of responsibility to other people, may I strongly

Monthly and Daily Guides: May

suggest that you keep this characteristic of yours strictly under control, otherwise you'll be in somebody's bad books before the day is through.

25 TUESDAY Cash-wise this seems to be a good positive day, and perhaps one when you should consider some long-term investments. What's more, your sex life is likely to be more important than usual and many of you will be developing some dramatic crushes; one attraction for you is basically due to your love of drama, which they, too, seem to possess.

26 WEDNESDAY You seem to be getting on better with people, including those awkward members of the family or your circle. Now, at last, you feel able to toss aside past differences because, Aries, you are the last person in the zodiac who will bear any kind of grudge – you're far too busy for that. Your behaviour could make somebody close to you a lot happier and more at ease. Enjoy the period of calm because, let's face it, we don't get too many of them, do we?

27 THURSDAY This seems to be a day when you are in the throes of sorting out some very mixed and confused emotions. Luckily, the stars will be providing you with a time when it will be relatively easy to discard negative influences that have been troubling you for some time, and free yourself for a more relaxed and secure life on the personal front. This evening is a good time for taking up new pursuits.

28 FRIDAY Many of you will have been considering making more important changes in a relationship and, if so, this is a good time to leap into action. Don't hesitate, because the person you care about will certainly be receptive to your ideas and your feelings, so there's no danger of your sensitive pride being damaged, even to the slightest degree. Put your best foot forward then.

29 SATURDAY The stars suggest it would be a good idea to at least think about making minor adjustments to your ambitions, and also to mix business with pleasure whenever the opportunity arises. You'll certainly find that workmates and colleagues will get on like a house on fire with your loved ones at home. This will help consolidate your work relationships, and will make it a good deal easier for you to extract favours from them on the professional front whenever the need arises.

30 SUNDAY There's a strong likelihood that you'll be doing plenty of positive work in the background of things instead of the limelight, which in general is your choice. If you're involved in any intense activity then progress is going to be remarkably swift. What's more, although you may sense a feeling of tension between people you are visiting today, on no account should you interfere – of course, if they seek your advice then it's different, but do wait to be asked.

31 MONDAY At work you are in a helpful and cooperative mood for much of the day. You aren't selfish by nature, and you will be seriously trying to help somebody else. Your own talents will be obvious and in your personal life you will be optimistic. This evening you may have to look after someone else's welfare or belongings, and this could make you anxious.

JUNE

In June the Sun will be floating along in the airy sign of Gemini up until the 20th, and this is the area of your chart involved with communication with other people, short trips, brothers and sisters. This is a time when you can easily put your point across to other people so don't hesitate to do just that.

On the 21st, the Sun will be moving into the water sign of Cancer, the area of your chart devoted to home and property. It looks as if you'll be entertaining in your own nest rather than straying too far to find fun and games. Also, it's a good time for making decisions on the part of the family.

Mercury will be in Taurus for the first five days of the month and it's likely you might be signing an important document in connection with your job, or perhaps being asked to take a trip. On the 6th Mercury moves into Gemini, so again, communication with others will go swimmingly. It stays in this position up until the 20th when it moves into Cancer and that, of course, is the area of your chart devoted to the home, where there seems to be quite a lot of movement going on and decisions being made.

Venus is in Gemini all month but is in an awkward mood, and is in retrograde movement up until 28 June. It wouldn't be a good idea then to make any important decisions until this silly planet sees sense once more.

Mars is in Cancer until the 23rd, and so there could be some tension and squabbles on the home front. If you have children you'd best protect them when in the kitchen or the bathroom, as little accidents and scalds are a possibility – do take care and you'll have nothing to fear.

On the 24th, Mars moves on into the sign of Leo and the area of your chart devoted to sport, children, creativity and social life. Unfortunately, however, it will be easy for you to fall out with other people because Mars can be an aggressive planet, as you know. Protect your children too – they may be a little bit more robust and energetic than is usually the case. There's nothing wrong with this month at all, just as long as you're a little bit more thoughtful and caring where the family are concerned. This done, you can relax.

The pattern made by the stars during June seems to emphasize that there's a lot of to-ing and fro-ing going on and whilst doing so you'll meet lots of new faces, which will liven up your life quite considerably.

1 TUESDAY Today, unusually so, you won't insist on always being the leader: you're prepared to listen to other people's points of view and you are gaining respect in a positive way. This evening you'll want to get out and try your hand at something different, and so if a friend or neighbour suggests an activity you've never tried before, then why not be a bit of a devil and experiment – this is certainly a good day for doing just that.

2 WEDNESDAY There are most certainly times when you feel like breaking the rules and rebelling, what fire sign doesn't? Of course, when this happens, no-one can stop you when this mood is upon you. However, today you'll find it difficult to come to terms with developments in your personal life but, whatever you do, you must avoid bottling up your emotions. If you do keep everything inside, your loved ones may think that you don't care and nothing could be further from the truth. In actual fact, this is a rare mood you seem to be in because as a rule, with Aries people, everybody knows exactly what they are thinking and feeling.

3 THURSDAY This is the day of the Full Moon and it occurs in the fiery sign of Sagittarius – that's the area of your chart devoted to foreign affairs, legal matters and higher education. You may have to adapt to somebody else's ideas, so at least give them a listen before you turn them down. If you don't, I'm afraid any of you involved in legal tussles could come out as losers.

4 FRIDAY Today you are provided with a period for serious decisions and also for sorting out problems and making your thoughts known to those who are closest to you. Furthermore, it's a good time for smoothing over differences between friends and family and generally introducing a theme of common sense wherever you may be. The influence of an older or more experienced person could also be important, so if you brush aside their ideas and suggestions you'll realize at a later date that you may have made a big mistake.

5 SATURDAY Although this day may be a hard-working one, you'll be deriving a great deal of enjoyment out of it too. It's likely, for example, that workmates may be inviting you to join them on some social occasion, or if your luck is really in, there's a possibility that they may be making a romantic approach. Whether you fancy them or not, this certainly will be providing you with an ego boost, but if you do need to turn them down, do make sure that you do so with a certain amount of charm and courtesy, won't you?

6 SUNDAY Today Mercury will be moving into Gemini and this livens up your imagination as well as your grey cells, and also keeps you on the go in a physical sense. You're going to be good company this evening so keep a high profile and get out with your friends; you'll make them laugh and you'll go to bed tonight feeling that you've thoroughly enjoyed yourself, and everybody will have enjoyed your company too.

7 MONDAY If you need any favours or are hoping to make an impression on the opposite sex today, do think twice before leaping into action. It's important that you make this day count in some way, because you could regret it at a later date if you just let it pass by. It's a great time for presenting your creative ideas to other people; they're certainly going to be well received and your loved ones seem to be in a caring mood.

8 TUESDAY There's sure to be a relaxing influence around the home and family, as tension lifts and you begin to see the way clear in domestic matters much more sensibly. You know you can never let yourself become trapped or tied down by the endless details of life, as you have in the past, but simply realizing this will help you to feel that things are finally on the up, which they most definitely are.

9 WEDNESDAY Should you want a time for sorting out matters connected with creativity, sports, arts or children, this is it. If not, simply give yourself over to romance. If you are carrying a torch for somebody, this could be the time for letting them know how you feel.

10 THURSDAY You're feeling more positive and inspired about the future. Your pleasure-seeking impulses are strong but need to be kept in the bounds of reason, because it's not out of the question that you could go completely over the top, spending too much money, eating too much rich food and making love

Monthly and Daily Guides: June

until you're completely exhausted. But I can think of worse ways to spend your time.

11 FRIDAY This is a time when you mustn't take anything for granted where cash matters are concerned. Situations will be changing on the hour, every hour, so there's no point in making hard and fast decisions for the time being. Wait until the dust has settled – then you will know exactly what your next move should be. Ignore petty arguments within the family; let relatives get on with their own differences because you really can't do any good by poking your nose in.

12 SATURDAY It seems that one friendship is providing you with enough fun and pleasure to make up for difficulties you have been experiencing in your intimate circles for quite a while. Today make certain that you keep on the move, but be careful not to overdo it or you could become hyperactive. If you're totally clear and straightforward, you will soon be in a position to see your popularity soar through the roof.

13 SUNDAY There seems to be a certain amount of strain between yourself and another person over money. Certainly, if someone is wasting your hard-earned cash you have a right to know why, but on the other hand they're spending their own money too. Quite frankly, it's entirely up to you to sort this matter out. Lastly, watch your possessions if you're out and about in crowds this evening.

14 MONDAY The stars today certainly help you to make a good impression and you can rest assured that this trend will go on for a couple of days or so. You're beginning to gather your courage to sweep away the old cobwebs without having to get rid of things or people you really value and whom you want to hang on to. Nevertheless, it is vital to give yourself elbow-room and not let yourself be hurried or hassled.

15 TUESDAY Behind the scenes you are still struggling to sort out some kind of complex emotional situation. It might be wise to proceed very slowly and cautiously, with the knowledge that at the end of the day you will triumph better than you could have expected. There is good news, too, on the horizon – perhaps small presents will be coming your way, or it may be that a brief moment of enlightenment proves to be satisfying.

16 WEDNESDAY In your work other people will be introducing fresh faces to you who can help fulfil your wishes and dreams in the very near future, because they possess the specialized knowledge that you need so badly. It may be time for pocketing your pride but, if so, you won't live to regret it, so why not give it a whirl?

17 THURSDAY Today is the day when there is a nice New Moon in Gemini, and it looks as if there could be an impromptu get-together with siblings or neighbours which is sure to delight you. If there has been a wrangle with a brother or sister, take this golden opportunity to extend an olive branch. If you don't, you'll be kicking yourself, I can assure you.

18 FRIDAY Your popularity at work is not in question and people will be falling over themselves to do you favours. Invitations come through people you meet whilst going about the daily grind and many of you will be mixing business with pleasure and this could, at a later date, lead to romance. Creative work can be launched in a big way.

19 SATURDAY There may be an unreal feel about the day and situations you find yourself in. It won't pay for you to take anything for granted, and instead you should do a little investigating. Muddles that do crop up can be cleared away with a bit of common sense; the question is, do you have any of this commodity left?

20 SUNDAY Flirting with acquaintances or just having a touch of gentle fun is helping you to take the strain out of the day, but don't start feeling guilty and blaming yourself for all the recent upheavals in your life. You can't be in charge of all circumstances all the time, even though ideally you would like this to be the case. If somebody suggests an unexpected approach, be open minded because, let's face it, you're strongly drawn to originality.

21 MONDAY Today is the day when the Sun will be moving into Cancer and that is the area of your chart devoted to home, family and property. Therefore, if you want to make any big changes then discuss these with your partner; they are likely to concur with your wishes, so for a change there won't be any battles or wrangling over who is going to get their own way.

22 TUESDAY You've done your best to make sure that you are seen as sparkling, charismatic, different and outgoing. The result is that you are having much more fun now than you have had for a while. No doubt there are days and times when you have to be practical, but this is not one of them. Just be sure that you are allowing everyone to understand how you feel.

23 WEDNESDAY Today you can expect a certain amount of muddle and confusion, even mystery, both at work and at home. The best thing to do is not to take anything or anyone for granted and, worst of all, take situations and people at face value. There's a good deal going on beneath the surface here, Aries, and it's up to you to find out exactly what's going on, otherwise you'll fall into a trap.

24 THURSDAY Today your ruling planet, Mars, will be moving into Leo and you will take on, temporarily anyway, some of the characteristics of this sign, becoming much more proud and insisting on having your own way. Luckily there's also a credit side in as much as you'll be much more generous, feeling and loving. This is a happy period for you, but at a later date you'll wonder what on earth came over you.

25 FRIDAY If you're not careful you could waste money on a whim or through carelessness. Avoid getting into a financial discussion with loved ones because the air is thick with tension and a great deal may be said and done which will be regretted at a later date. If taken to the point of extreme, a relationship may even come to an end, so beware.

26 SATURDAY A certain amount of disagreement and upset could be happening on the home front. This may be due to the fact that while you're concentrating on realizing your ambitions you are neglecting those at home, or a social occasion may not live up to its high expectations, or there may be a disappointment in connection with property.

27 SUNDAY Kind messages put you in a sentimental mood and there may even be a proposition coming your way too which will do your morale a world of good. Certainly a close partner is in a mood for fun and may spring a few surprises on you. Keep cool and don't be too possessive. You can at least allow yourself the luxury of taking it easy a little bit, but don't take things to extremes.

28 MONDAY Today is the day when Venus resumes direct movement so relationships, socializing and sporting events should all be less complicated than they have for quite some time. This means that you can make a few minor changes, providing, of course, that you consult your partner. Having done this all should be well.

29 TUESDAY If you're making money or simply spending it (and, let's face it, you're good at both), you are determined to have your fair share of the fun – and why not? But do remember that one close partner is not in a position to be generous, so what you give away will just have to made up for by yourself, and it may not be as easy as it sounds. At work feel free to follow your own inclinations and be a good deal more upbeat.

30 WEDNESDAY There could be a falling out with somebody today. Naturally you can't allow yourself to be bullied or coerced, but on the other hand neither should you be deliberately awkward or perverse simply for the sake of some kind of power struggle. If an emotional relationship has been going through a rocky phase, this could very well be the day when it is called to a halt.

JULY

The Sun this month will be floating along in the water sign of Cancer up until the 21st of the month and that, of course, is the area of your chart devoted to home and family. You're going to be much more domesticated than is usually the case. Friends may wonder what on earth is going on, but you're enjoying all of the warmth of the family. On the 22nd, the Sun moves into Leo, a fire sign like your good self, and the good times are upon you. It's great for creativity, matters related to children, casual romance and generally pleasing yourself.

Mercury will be in Cancer for the first four days of the month, so this would be a good time for signing any necessary documents, especially in connection with property affairs. On the 5th, Mercury also moves into fiery Leo, and there seems to be quite a lot of minor changes taking place in your social life and where matters related to children are concerned too. If you're at all creative this is a very fruitful time.

On 26 July, Mercury will be moving into Virgo. You seem to be stuck in routine from hereon in – well, for a couple of days or so anyway – and there's nothing you can do about it. Just get prepared to catch up on work that may have been neglected.

Venus will be in Gemini all month and if you've any members of this sign in your circle you'll be seeing and hearing a lot from them. They may even be making interesting introductions if you happen to be fancy free, but if you're not then don't be naughty.

Mars will be in Leo all month, therefore, you need to take care when taking part in any kind of sport. You're somewhat accident prone, and the same applies to your love life – you 'think' you're in love, but basically it's all in your imagination. Don't humour yourself; just wait and see what happens rather than going completely mad.

The pattern made by the stars in July places a great deal of emphasis on family affairs and the sign of Cancer. If you have anyone in your circle born under this sign they'll be extremely helpful to you. Furthermore, it is a time for introspection rather than being too gregarious and outgoing; if you become too outrageous other people will consider that you are completely mad and, quite frankly, I wouldn't blame them. All in all then, it looks to be an interesting, if somewhat confusing month.

1 THURSDAY You'll probably find it difficult to remember the last time you were in a strong enough position to call the shots and influence events, either in your emotional life or at work. However, with the planetary activity in your chart at this moment in time it isn't a period to be afraid to ask for what you want.

2 FRIDAY The month kicks off with a somewhat sour note because there is a Full Moon in the sign of Capricorn. If you've anybody in your circle born under this sign it might be a good idea to avoid them for the time being as they're going to be tetchy, bad tempered and uncooperative. However, it is a good time for putting the finishing touches to work, relationships or anything else in your life, so don't hesitate to do that at least.

3 SATURDAY You'll be quite surprised when others give you your way without a second thought. This evening, you want to be out locally. Somebody you meet by chance will put a good thing your way, possibly romantically, but more likely in connection with your ambitions and work.

4 SUNDAY The old grey matter is whizzing around these days, and it's a wonder you don't have steam coming out of your ears. Your brain is full to bursting with no end of original thoughts, any one of which could make your life a good deal fuller and richer. Even so, there is a limit to the amount of support you can expect from other people. Mind you, as an Aries, you prefer to carve out your own fate anyway, so this is unlikely to faze you one little bit. This evening looks good for brief encounters.

5 MONDAY Today is the day when Mercury will be moving into the fire sign of Leo. This is the sign that rules matters related to creativity, children, casual romance and the good times in your chart. There may be some small changes in connection with such affairs but, all in all, you've precious little to worry about.

6 TUESDAY The combination of the planets gives you a sparkling aspect today. This will be providing a touch of magic to your creative work and ideas. Generally speaking you have a great deal of confidence, but for some reason you are hesitating about approaching other people. Come on, Aries, you're known for your bravado, so put your best foot forward and get cracking.

7 WEDNESDAY There could be one or two surprises coming from friends or acquaintances. What they have to say will be illuminating as well as unusual, but it will give you plenty of food for thought.

8 THURSDAY Though already fairly busy you will have to hold on to your hat as life speeds up even more. The words will slide out helter-skelter, whether you are writing letters or on the phone, or just talking your way through the day. Short journeys will occupy you, and I think it might be a good idea for you to plan for a rather scattered routine.

Monthly and Daily Guides: July

9 FRIDAY Friends and acquaintances are certainly in high spirits; they're also at their most sociable and probably extending invitations. If you need their advice on any matter at all, then you have an ideal day for picking their brains, or at least getting their opinions. What you hear will not only be helpful, but also is likely to please you.

10 SATURDAY Today you'll be inclined to spend without due thought. You may decide to give in to this and, of course, the decision is yours, but it might be a good idea to draw in your financial horns for the time being.

11 SUNDAY The planetary set-up today suggests that if you need to hit a target quickly, then you have any number of arrows in your quiver to choose from. But having so many choices can also lead to confusion, particularly for you, so keep things simple and tackle one thing at a time and then you can achieve and accomplish more than you would have imagined.

12 MONDAY Other people are trying to prove their dominance by being extra demanding, but you will be equally awkward by remaining true to your proposals and refusing to budge. Try to work towards an acceptable compromise if at all possible – and it really should be.

13 TUESDAY A show of strength in your working environment will turn fantasy into reality where hopes and dreams are concerned. The never-ending roller-coaster of work will gradually de-accelerate into a steady pace, but you need to think on your feet when making negotiations for your financial security in the future.

♈

14 WEDNESDAY Your inspirational creativity opens up a whole new world of options in your career, but there is no time to procrastinate. Speed is of the essence when the sign points you in the right direction, so adopt a no nonsense approach and you'll go from strength to strength.

15 THURSDAY Today there will be some fresh opportunities for meeting new people and having fun, so make sure you're looking your best. Stretch out the hand of friendship and you'll be glad that you did, because it could lead to romance.

16 FRIDAY This is a day for making sensible decisions. It's also a time when you'll be getting some good advice from contacts. The only question is, Aries, are you going to listen?

17 SATURDAY Today is the day of the New Moon and it falls in the watery sign of Cancer, once again the area of your chart devoted to home and property affairs. If you're negotiating perhaps trying to buy a new house you couldn't have picked a better time. It's a great evening for socializing with close buddies who will certainly appreciate all the efforts you put out on their part. As always with New Moons it's a good time for making fresh starts.

18 SUNDAY Changes at work have led to shifts in the balance of power, but you'll feel secure in the knowledge that you've made the right choices. Dramatic developments in your personal life encourage a more stable situation.

19 MONDAY Your perceptions, experience and logic will be put to the test when the stars ask you to ensure that you are on the right path. Saying goodbye to the past may have to include

Monthly and Daily Guides: July

family members too. Nevertheless, you should adopt unbridled enthusiasm and keep moving forward.

20 TUESDAY Financial reward for ground work done in the past now begins to come through, and a delicious feeling of anticipation over what can now be achieved will leave you feeling better. Make sure you are aware of your own worth.

21 WEDNESDAY Avoid the idea of everyone having a hidden agenda because you never know, a happy event may be spoilt by your nosiness. Keep yourself to yourself and don't take things to heart. Sometimes a situation looks one way at the moment of impact, but further down the line it assumes a different hue.

22 THURSDAY Today is the day when the Sun will be moving into the area of your chart which represents children, creativity, the good times and casual romance – the fiery sign of Leo. So get out your dancing shoes and enjoy yourself.

23 FRIDAY Friendship and joint efforts are under the microscope today. Make this a time when loved ones prove their worth; those not made of the right stuff will buckle at the knees when put to the test. Don't be afraid to take an independent stance or put yourself in the spotlight. You'll have the capacity to rise to the occasion and change people's opinions of your talents.

24 SATURDAY Career matters are to the fore and now could be the right time for a major ambition to be realized, even if you don't think you have any particular aspirations. If you think deep down inside yourself I think you'll find that you have.

This is a time for being a little bit more daring, after all, what have you got to lose? Not a great deal.

25 SUNDAY Today you need to be as adventurous as possible. Forget about your usual haunts and go out and explore new terrain. The further you travel, or the more you mix with unfamiliar faces, the more stimulated your mind is going to be. Your family may make unrealistic demands on your time and energy and you may have to make a firm stand. Do not allow yourself to be bullied.

26 MONDAY Today the stars seem to be concerned with your health, well-being and work. The cluster of planets is in a powerful combination and this will help you. Getting in shape and sorting out unfinished business is going to be par for the course right now. If you are happy with the way things are, tread carefully, otherwise you can respond to powerful undercurrents by making revolutionary moves.

27 TUESDAY This is a creative and social, perhaps romantic, time. Invitations to weddings and other celebrations should be piling up. There's also a chance that you may experience a major breakthrough, or be presented with some welcome event. It's worth giving your all in every situation – after all, it's what you don't do that you'll end up regretting, not what you did.

28 WEDNESDAY This is a time when you will be tempted to spend an above-average amount of money on your home. However, hopefully someone close will be able to restrain you if you are about to go overboard. Be sure to stick to a budget if you have one. If not, it might be a good idea to put one into operation now.

29 THURSDAY You may have itchy feet and you'll have more than one chance to exercise them soon – this is a time for getting up and going. Communications of every description are in the spotlight and you will need to exercise a great deal of care and patience with other people.

30 FRIDAY The stars seem to be energizing team work as well as your circle of friends. It's also possible that those buddies of yours may be trying to interest you in a member of the opposite sex. However, regardless of what they say, believe you me, the relationship is likely to be purely physical rather than anything else, so don't get carried away.

31 SATURDAY Today is the day of the Full Moon and it occurs in the airy sign of Aquarius. This is the section of your chart devoted to team work and club activities and someone could be going out of their way to be awkward. Try not to rise to the bait but don't shrink from letting them know that being part of a team means just that!

AUGUST

The Sun this month will be sizzling away through the fiery sign of Leo up until the 22nd. There seems to be a great emphasis on creativity, matters related to children, casual romance and, generally speaking, the light-hearted side to life. Make the most of this period, especially if you are going on holiday – you've certainly picked a good time too.

On the 23rd, the Sun will be moving into Virgo so you'll have to be a little bit more serious now. Maybe work has been neglected for quite some time and now you are expected to catch up; if so, don't hesitate to do so.

Mercury is in Virgo up until the 24th, but turns retrograde on 10 August. So there are going to be minor changes on the working front, not that they are all going to appeal to you I'm afraid, because what is being suggested or put forward is purely routine and all you can do is go along with what is being said. After all, life cannot be one gigantic party, even though that would be rather nice, wouldn't it?

Mercury will be also moving back into Leo on the 25th, so this will galvanize matters related to creativity, children, sports and casual romance. There seems to be a good deal of fun going on at this time, which is nice, but do make sure you double check all the arrangements, or you could miss out.

Venus will be in Gemini during the first week, throwing a rosy glow over short journeys and casual romance. If you've already got a partner in tow, for heaven's sake resist attractive members of the opposite sex because, believe you me, somebody's going to let your other half know exactly what's going on. Well, there's always a busybody around somewhere, isn't there?

On the 7th, Venus will be moving into Cancer, making life a good deal easier on the home front, and it looks as if you'll be socializing a great deal more than is usually the case. However, life perhaps won't be quite as adventurous as you might like. Nevertheless, bathe in the glory and admiration of your family.

Your ruling planet, Mars, will be in Leo during the first week or so of August, so you could be impetuous in at least one area of life and perhaps even two. Those hormones are coursing through your veins, so if you are married you've got to be sensible, or else there's going to be a hell of a lot of trouble later on.

Mars moves on into Virgo on the 10th, so now you can channel that energy into sheer hard work and take your eyes off the opposite sex – especially if they are 'forbidden'. Well,

Aries, you can't always have your own way although it would be nice for you I've got to admit; nevertheless, there are plenty of good times ahead so don't worry.

The pattern made by the stars in August places the emphasis on introspection and planning rather than the pleasurable sides to life. If you do meet up with people it's likely to be on your own base. It very much seems as if you, and perhaps your partner, have got important decisions to make and you need plenty of time and elbow room in which to do this. Nevertheless, once you have reached your conclusions you can then heave a sigh of relief and get out and let off a bit of steam – you're certainly going to need to do so at this time. With any luck, bearing in mind the month we are in, there may be a chance for you to take at least a weekend break with that special person, and if you do, you'll come back replenished and ready to get stuck back into life once more.

1 SUNDAY For the time being at least you can take it easy. It's likely the stars have thrown you into an awkward situation and now you need time to think things through. Fortunately, you have some friends who are very much on your side and you'll be getting some good advice; it's up to you to decide whether it's worth taking.

2 MONDAY Something, or someone, is beginning to irritate the hell out of you. Each time you try to muster some enthusiasm, respond to a sense of hope or generally attempt any kind of positive new move, you run straight into a brick wall. There is, it seems, a reason why you can't, or mustn't, move at this moment in time, partly linked to the fact that freedom isn't quite as easy to obtain just now.

3 TUESDAY People always want what they haven't got – it's human nature. There's only one thing more attractive than an apple that's just out of reach and that's forbidden fruit. The stars are intensifying your hunger and a deep meaningful experience of something pleasurable and different seems to be on the horizon. The stars are helpful and trying to tell you fulfillment of this need is not out of the question.

4 WEDNESDAY Freedom is a wonderful idea. But true freedom, however, involves the freedom to choose to accept restraint. If we really can do anything we want, we wind up lacking purpose and thus our identity seems to pall. All things are possible so why do anything different? What you want now is a very specific form of freedom from a particular thing or situation. The stars suggest you can have it, but just before you try to strive for it, take time to consider – what will you then have to kick against?

5 THURSDAY For the past few days a combination of demanding situations and tack has meant keeping a low profile about certain important issues. The Moon has now shifted enough and not only should you be able to say what you think, but it would also be wise to do so.

6 FRIDAY You appear to be in an awkward position through no fault of your own, but there's no way out of it without confronting issues. By detailing problems without placing the blame at anyone's doorstep you can transform awkward situations into ones that resolve persistent difficulties.

7 SATURDAY Today is the day when Venus will be entering Cancer and that's the area of your chart devoted to home, so things look as if they are calming down a little bit and you may even be socializing on the home front, which will impress everybody who comes calling. Furthermore, if you want to improve your homestead this is a good time for making moves to do so.

8 SUNDAY Once you realize that reason has nothing to do with the approach others are taking to the puzzles you now face, things become considerably clearer. This then allows you to take off the kid gloves and make statements that leave no doubt about your views and your preferences.

9 MONDAY Although you're not sentimental by nature you are probably still finding it difficult to say goodbye to certain elements of the past. Curiously what you now seem so hard to part with could become a burden as you enter the new chapter of life the stars are placing before you.

10 TUESDAY Today Mercury goes into retrograde movement and so it certainly isn't a good time for trading in the car, running from place to place or signing important documents. Leave these for at least a week or so, whenever you 'feel' life is going to be kinder to you.

11 WEDNESDAY Mars has moved into Virgo now – the area of your chart devoted to health. Therefore, you need to be especially careful where sharp and hot objects are concerned. If anyone's going to run across a mishap I'm afraid it's going to be you. It shouldn't be anything too serious, but do take care, including, of course, when you are on the road.

12 THURSDAY You may once have thought that certain issues related to family, domesticity or property matters would never be settled, but now they are on their way to resolution. Once these are finally behind you, your focus can return to previously sidelined activities of a more appealing nature.

13 FRIDAY Often what initially seems ridiculous, illogical or unreasonable could, in the long run, be in your best interest. Keep this in mind as you decide whether to go along with unsettling proposals or unexpected changes that would completely revolutionize your working life or daily routine.

14 SATURDAY There's likely to be the beginning of a new cycle where routine work is concerned or perhaps where a relationship needs attention. Either way, you seem to have a lot to look forward to and may even be combining business with pleasure during this particular evening.

15 SUNDAY Being straightforward by nature, your honesty is valued by friends. This time, however, you seem to have been too bold in your statements of the truth, so it would be wise to smooth ruffled feathers of certain individuals before you go any further.

16 MONDAY This is the day of the New Moon and it occurs in the fiery sign of Leo so it looks as if there are going to be quite a few changes in connection with matters related to children, casual romance and creativity. If you're hoping somebody is going to improve your efforts on the working front then I don't think you're going to be disappointed.

17 TUESDAY You may have been holding back from making any lasting commitments until you were sure which way a loved one was going. However less sincere their declarations

Monthly and Daily Guides: August

are, changes that occur now are bound to alter their plans and, in turn, your destiny.

18 WEDNESDAY There seems to be some tension with a colleague, but resist the temptation to lay down the law. Everyone has their own unique contribution to make, not just you, Aries!

19 THURSDAY It seems you have been debating the pros and cons of your choices endlessly, yet every effort to get things underway has been frustrated. If you can just be patient for a few days longer, events themselves will force those who are being indecisive to act.

20 FRIDAY It may seem ridiculous to stand your ground over matters when you know that changes are coming in a few days. Nevertheless, it will be unwise to give the impression that you will go along with any attitude or proposal that goes against your beliefs.

21 SATURDAY Confrontation is the last resort for you, because you consider yourself to have failed if you cannot bring about some kind of resolution, preferably in your favour. However, it is worth considering that certain people may respond only when situations have reached crisis level.

22 SUNDAY This is likely to be a peaceful Sunday. You want to get away from the madding crowd so are quite happy to put your feet up in front of the television or involve yourself in a good book. If others wish to disturb your peace by asking you out unexpectedly, you should politely decline as this is an ideal time for recharging your batteries and thinking of what you need or want from the future.

23 MONDAY Today is the day when the Sun will be moving into Virgo the area of your chart devoted to health and hard work. Life won't be quite as frivolous as it has of late, nevertheless, you're going to get a great deal done and this will be satisfying in itself. Those of you with Virgos in your life may be in for quite a few surprises in their direction.

24 TUESDAY Patience and persistence are qualities that you need to cultivate right now, they have been severely tested recently particularly through friends and workmates. Nevertheless, it looks as if you're about to come out on top now and you can relax and look forward to making a few changes in your life.

25 WEDNESDAY You will be very casual in your approach to other people today. Certainly you will be drawn to friendships, but without the need for personal ties. Unconventional activities could also stir your imagination, and because of this you are likely to be taking on a new activity or hobby. You will be more than happy to give advice to close contacts where it is needed.

26 THURSDAY Mercury has moved into Leo now, a fire sign like your good self, but unfortunately in retrograde motion. You may be asked to sign some kind of contract in connection with work but try to put it off until next month. Expect delays if travelling for professional reasons. Those who are gadding about locally are likely to meet an interesting face from the past that could turn into a friend. However, if you've got a partner, of course, you'd better be careful: somebody may gossip and let drop that they've seen you flirting with somebody else – well, you know what other people are like, don't you?

27 FRIDAY A lack of feedback from other people can be dispiriting and whatever they say could be easily misinterpreted as a direct refusal. But it would be unwise to see this silence or uncommunicative mood of loved ones as rejection, when all it signifies is that they are temporarily distracted.

28 SATURDAY Unnecessary worries about money or other practicalities are indicated by the stars on this particular day. However, because you usually have an abundance of intuition some of these concerns could prove to be well worth investigating.

29 SUNDAY You may run across a stroke of good luck whilst going about your everyday tasks, so keep your eyes and ears open because to allow them to pass you by would be something you would regret, if not now then in the future.

30 MONDAY Today is the day of the Full Moon and it falls in the sign of Pisces. This is the area of your chart which represents behind the scene intrigues, so it could be that there's quite a lot of scandal-mongering going on in your friendships, or perhaps work. Do keep alert and make sure that somebody isn't trying to do you down; it's possible that they may be jealous of your recent successes and you don't want to be the last one to know about this. It's always nice to know who are our friends and who are not.

31 TUESDAY Sometimes there's a logical explanation for the tides of emotions, but the planetary movement today explains why partners or those close to us have been upset and this will give a rare insight into their true feelings. Don't be surprised if you don't like what you hear or see – sometimes we cannot control other people and that happens to be most of the time, doesn't it?

SEPTEMBER

The Sun this month is digging its way through the earthy sign of Virgo up until the 22nd, and as far as you are concerned this tends to relate to yourself, your daily routine and your relationships with workmates. Should you be feeling a little under the weather then do be kind to yourself. As an Aries, you often 'over-stretch' yourself and this is a time for recognizing this fault and doing something practical about it.

On the 23rd, the Sun will be moving into Libra which, of course, is your opposite sign, and so the emphasis over the next few weeks is going to be on your relationships with other people, both for good and bad. Nevertheless, you are generally a fairly popular person; the only problem is that you always over-ride other people's feelings. You don't do this consciously but, nevertheless, it can cause a certain amount of trouble, so do try to control this.

What about changeable Mercury? It certainly has been playing up recently, not only confusing us but itself too. Luckily it resumes direct movement on the 2nd and is pushing ahead through the days until it moves into Virgo on the 10th. Virgo, of course, is representative of work where minor changes are taking place and new faces may be entering the scene, but just for once you don't feel threatened by this and you make sure that there is a warm welcome waiting for anybody new. You're not silly, after all, and you may as well get them on your side now.

Venus is in Cancer during the first week and while this state of affairs exists there's a great deal of cosiness and warmth on the home front. Those of you who are connected with property matters should be doing exceptionally well.

On the 7th, Venus will be moving into Leo where it stays for the remainder of the month. This will help you reach out into life. If you have any foreign connections you could be getting in touch with them or vice versa, or perhaps you're making new friends on a social level and, if so, this will broaden your horizons as well as your social circle, so that you'll be feeling pretty good about yourself and your life in general.

Mars will be in Virgo up until 25 September, which is the area of your chart devoted to sheer hard slog. I'm afraid you are going to have to put your shoulder to the wheel if you are to achieve anything at all. Furthermore, remember that this is also the area of your chart devoted to health and because you are invariably in a hurry cuts, bruises and minor accidents are all possibilities. All you need to do is be a little bit more thoughtful and careful and you will have precious little to worry about.

On the 26th, Mars will be leaping into your opposite sign of Libra where it stays for the remainder of the month. Other people are going to be a little bit tetchy so don't push them beyond reasonable boundaries otherwise you're going to regret it.

The pattern made by the stars seems to be placing the emphasis on home life, property and entertaining rather than being too adventurous which, of course, is usually the case. Never mind, you'll be getting closer to those people who really count because of this attitude and other people may even be introducing new people so that your friendship circle will also widen too. Property matters are also well starred and if you're thinking of buying a flat or a home then push ahead as quickly as you can during this month because a great deal can be achieved.

All in all, things look to be promising so be quick to take advantage.

1 WEDNESDAY Right now no-one has a clearer sense of their objectives, but even you can benefit from a little self doubt. In fact, the insights that accompany today's planetary action could resolve a long unanswered question.

2 THURSDAY Today Mercury finally resumes direct movement and so the confusion over paperwork, travelling, the car and little irritations in general should begin to evaporate. I bet you'll be pretty pleased about this!

3 FRIDAY You should be feeling more confident and able to handle challenges more deftly now. In fact, in this fast-paced day, surprises and even setbacks can be turned to your advantage, so push ahead.

4 SATURDAY It's not easy to make a difficult decision as most of us realize, especially when you need to find yourself having immediately to justify yourself. Do the best you can to keep in mind that those questioning you are unlikely to be any more sure of their facts than you are.

5 SUNDAY At times of movement and change, the expectation for you to make a major commitment is likely to set you up for a disappointment, no matter how reasonable what has already been agreed upon may seem. Don't be surprised if you have to make even more substantial changes over the next couple of days.

6 MONDAY Your tolerance may be wearing thin with individuals who seem to think rules of right and wrong don't apply to them, but just hang on in there. The pendulum will swing so that by next week these circumstances that permitted such arrogance will, instead, condemn it.

7 TUESDAY Today is the day when Venus will be moving into Leo and while this planet is so situated your social life and your love life are certainly going to be fun. Furthermore, if you're at all creative, then you'll be getting any kind of back up that you need to push ahead with ideas, so don't be afraid to ask for such help because it will be forthcoming. This placing of Venus in Leo, of course, is extremely beneficial for sports, romance and really anything your little heart desires, so get out into life – this is certainly a good period for you.

8 WEDNESDAY Today is full of changes – some welcome, others less so – and it would be naïve to expect friends, colleagues or family to stick to plans. It's possible that they may be justified by complaining for one reason or another. It might be a good idea to sit down and have a serious talk.

9 THURSDAY Those of you who live, or work, with others may have found them reticent to discuss issues or their feelings, but don't force anything. As tensions build it will become more difficult for them to stay silent until eventually situations themselves compel them to say what's on their mind.

10 FRIDAY Those at home, or colleagues at work, may still be unwilling to talk over concerns. Simply approach them again from a different angle. They are just as eager to resolve matters but need to clear up their misunderstandings before moving ahead with discussions.

11 SATURDAY Mercury's moved on into Virgo and that's the area of your chart devoted to your relationship with workmates, which should now be pretty good, paperwork in connection with your career and, to a degree, daily routine. If you have a Virgo in your life they are likely to be in high spirits and this is the person to go to if you have any kind of problem.

12 SUNDAY Even when everything else is going well, you may face the choice of making an issue out of someone else's behaviour, or accepting things as they are. If a situation is getting you down then it might be a good idea to start thinking about making a few changes.

13 MONDAY There's a strong suggestion here that a minor new cycle is either beginning within an existing relationship, or that you are being introduced into a new circle of friends amongst whom you're likely to find a new admirer.

14 TUESDAY Today is the day of the New Moon and it occurs in the earthy sign of Virgo, which brings good news of constructive change on the working front, and your relationships with colleagues are improving too. However, there's a certain amount of stress where projects are concerned, so try to stay calm, take things slowly and you'll be able to work your way through matters without too much difficulty.

15 WEDNESDAY You seem to be backed into a corner by unpredictable circumstances which could prove to be difficult in practical terms and may cause serious doubts. The practicalities can wait until a little later, but the first step to conquering your doubts is to discuss them with uncharacteristic candour.

16 THURSDAY A change in pace is tiresome no matter what you're doing, but it becomes all the more tricky if issues involve money or joint ventures. Once you begin, however, you'll find that the momentum of developments themselves can carry things along, making it easier than you expected.

17 FRIDAY Measuring your feelings of relief that accompany the changes ushered in by today's stars, which accent partners, isn't easy. Last week you were beginning to resent others, viewing them as obstacles to progress; now you're recalling just how much fun it can really be.

18 SATURDAY You could be hesitant about taking chances, but with today's planetary set-up it would be foolish not to explore the opportunities coming your way. The indications are that you could be unrealistic to think everything would work out as expected.

19 SUNDAY For some time you have been putting off taking certain decisions but, though far from easy, they must be made. Now with such emphasis on the partnership area of your chart, the planets should light a fire under those who have been giving the impression that they can't be bothered.

20 MONDAY It might be a good idea to double-check all of your arrangements today: things seem to be a little bit chaotic and you might waste hours waiting around for people to turn up, ring or to contact you. Try to stay patient.

21 TUESDAY A friend may want a serious talk with you, perhaps they want to pick your brains, or maybe ask for advice. However, think before you give either unless you're certain that you really know what you're talking about, otherwise things could backfire at a later date.

22 WEDNESDAY The change in the stars heralds a new mood. This phase affects everyone, even the most stubborn, and you may find they will become more supportive and receptive to your ideas very soon.

23 THURSDAY Today is the day when the Sun will be moving into Libra and that is the area of your chart devoted to companionship in general, and in particular partnership, both professionally and in your private life. You, of course, always like to have your own way so you must remember we all must have our say from time to time; if you can do that you will not find yourself in anybody's bad books – see what you can do.

24 FRIDAY This is really not the time to attempt to use charm in order to attain your ends. Instead, you must try to convince others that you know your facts backwards. You may feel a little confused and uncertain about your personal life and long-term career issues. However, as you begin to take the initiative and tackle one problem at a time, then new chances will soon arrive which will help you to plan in a different direction and improve the quality of your life.

25 SATURDAY It would be easy to misinterpret today's opportunities as a product of someone's over-active imagination. However, not only should you take what they are offering seriously, but it could also lead to breakthroughs in personal and domestic matters which had, previously, brought only frustration.

26 SUNDAY Jupiter is now moving into your opposite sign of Libra, and there's certainly going to be a theme of cooperation and harmony over all of your relationships through the remainder of the year, which is nice, I think you'll agree.

27 MONDAY Mars is also now in Libra but fortunately not for too long, because Mars, of course, tends to be a quarrelsome planet and it could be stirring up trouble off and on where all of your relationships are concerned. One minute you're in favour with everyone, the next minute you are at the bottom of the popularity polls. Never mind, you can't win all the time, Aries, but do the best you can and perhaps other people will appreciate it, with any luck.

28 TUESDAY Today is the day of the Full Moon and it occurs in your sign, so you could get up feeling rather grumpy and bad tempered. Certainly it's not a time for pushing ahead with your usual pioneering spirit – wait until the Full Moon has done its worst, which is going to take a couple of days, then you can leap into action. In the meantime, be prepared to turn your attention elsewhere and wait for things to improve, which really won't take too long.

29 WEDNESDAY Today is the day when Mercury will be moving into Libra, so there are going to be new faces entering your scene, both at work, at home and when out enjoying yourself.

30 THURSDAY Today you must take into consideration the fact that other people may have some good ideas. Don't pinch them but, rather, give them some backing and they might ask you to join them. Whether you choose to take the sensible route just mentioned is entirely up to you, but if you're going to be 'stroppy' or envious, this could mean that the month will end on a very dodgy note.

OCTOBER

The Sun will be drifting along in the airy sign of Libra up until 22 October. This, of course, is your opposite number so like it or not you're going to have to defer to other people from time to time. Fortunately, though, if you happen to be without a partner, this could be that time of the year when you could be meeting various attractive members of the opposite sex and because of this – well, who knows what may happen?

The Sun will be moving into Scorpio on the 23rd and that's the area of your chart devoted to big business, insurance matters, club activities and, to a degree, friendship too. All of these can be well starred just as long as you don't insist on having your own way, which you do so often, don't you?

Mercury will be in Libra up until the 15th and other people will have some good ideas. You could be very popular when it comes to socializing, which is nice. However, once Mercury moves into Scorpio on the 16th there could be some trouble with the taxman, business matters and your relationships with colleagues. The best thing you can do is to make sure you are thorough in your work and then when it is time to sign off and escape the confines of your working environment get out into the big wide world in order to have fun. You're certainly going to need a couple of hours at the end of the day for 'letting rip',

Monthly and Daily Guides: October

and when you do so you will find that you can resume everyday life refreshed, ready to face the next day. So this can't be a bad ploy.

During October, Venus will be moving into Virgo on the 4th and that's the area of your chart devoted to working matters, which will be taking up a lot of your time. Nevertheless, new faces and ideas will prove to be stimulating so there's quite a lot to look forward to.

Venus will be moving into Libra on the 29th of the month and that, of course, is your opposite sign, so there is a definite happy glow over all relationships. When you are out partying, or socializing, strangers will become firm friends in record time. Furthermore, it's an excellent time for those of you who have been considering getting engaged or even married; if you are doing so during this particular month happiness is all but guaranteed.

Mars is in Libra all month so there could be a certain amount of tension from time to time. When you find yourself being unreasonable, and you're usually pretty good at recognizing this, accept the fact and make sure that you are thinking about other people's wants and needs as much as you think about your own. If you can do that then there'll be absolutely nothing wrong with this month whatsoever.

The pattern made by the stars this month suggests that you are thinking about other people more than is usually the case. Possibly in the past you have overlooked the wants and needs of people you've really cared about and maybe you've lost them and, if so, it looks as if a lesson has now been learnt and this is unlikely to happen again. Those of you who are dealing with legal matters should find that this is a lucky time, but that doesn't mean that you should become over-confident. Carry on sensibly and surely everything should be just fine.

1 FRIDAY No-one likes other people to make decisions for them, but especially not you, even though you are known for being a little bit pushy. Under normal circumstances it would seem wise to confront those who may be taking some kind of liberty, but with the current planetary set-up you are urged to go along with what is being proposed, at least for the time being.

2 SATURDAY You may not understand situations or cannot fathom what other people are on about, but don't wonder in silence. When entering a time of movement and change such as this, no-one is sure of everything and close associates may only be too happy to discuss matters, as well as welcome your ideas and guidance.

3 SUNDAY Frankly speaking, even at the best of times you can't always do what you want and today's planetary set-up indicates that if you try, you could become embroiled in a rather unpleasant power struggle and that simply isn't the way you like to live or work.

4 MONDAY Today is the day when Venus will be moving into Virgo and that's the area of your chart devoted to work and your relationships with people at a professional level. You will be able to charm others around to your way of thinking and your boss or your supervisor is certainly going to be pleased by your progress. In your personal life, if you happen to be involved with a Virgo, this is going to be an excellent time.

5 TUESDAY Don't keep what's on your mind a secret. Make your hopes and dreams clear and you'll be surprised how ready others are to make them a reality. You'll find it difficult

Monthly and Daily Guides: October

to stand your ground against certain individuals, but doing so now could enhance your self-esteem.

6 WEDNESDAY You're in for a frustrating day and one when you need to work twice as hard in order to gain the same ground. The last thing you need to do is to be disheartened because if you keep your shoulder to the wheel, you will eventually win through.

7 THURSDAY Friends and acquaintances seem to be a little bit tense and up-tight, therefore, if you need any favours it might be a good idea to postpone asking for them for at least 24 hours.

8 FRIDAY You may have right and reason on your side, but what you are faced with today could make it rather difficult. The best thing you can do is to stick to routine for the time being and all should be well.

9 SATURDAY This may not be the easiest of days in your life and difficult aspects indicate that there could be clashes with loved ones. However, you'll find explosive exchanges useful, not to clear the air, but to reveal information that would otherwise have been unnoticed.

10 SUNDAY You couldn't have a better day for discussions with people you are financially dependent upon, or perhaps sorting out financial matters such as tax. Naturally where the latter is concerned, you prefer to put your head in the sand, but in doing so you'll be storing up trouble for the future.

11 MONDAY You are likely to be adopting a much more serious attitude to your emotions and also to creative work. The influence of an older person can benefit you, as you are likely to be able to gain from their experience. Therefore, listen to what they have to say. It is likely that you will be rushed off your feet from morning to night but just remember, in order to remain healthy you also need to rest.

12 TUESDAY There are times when whatever you say or do, someone seems determined to raise objections. Therefore, search your conscience, review your plans and priorities and keep your decisions to yourself for the time being. Don't allow petty obstacles to deflate you from your chosen path.

13 WEDNESDAY If you have any important decisions to make, or perhaps you want to approach superiors or older people, then you have just the right day for doing so. When it comes to the emotional life, things could take a turn for the better, depending on your point of view, because it looks as if somebody wishes to alter a relationship and make it a good deal more committed.

14 THURSDAY Today is the day of the New Moon and it occurs in the airy sign of Libra. That's the area of your chart devoted to close partners and other people in general, which seems to be going along nicely. Even workmates and rivals are willing to help you out in any way they can, so this seems to be a good productive time. Push ahead.

15 FRIDAY Your hand is being forced by circumstances beyond your control and you're far from happy about it. However justified your feelings of anger or resentment may be, resist confronting those in charge until after you've had time to assess the situation and regain control of your temper.

Monthly and Daily Guides: October

16 SATURDAY Today Mercury will be moving into Scorpio, and the area of your chart devoted to big business, team effort and your relationships with workmates. There's a strong possibility you may have fallen out with somebody recently and if this should be the case, and you recognize the fact that you're both to blame, then it might be a good idea to take them out for a drink, or a meal, and smooth out your differences. You'll be feeling a good deal better and more productive after this.

17 SUNDAY After a very interesting, not to say inspiring, couple of days things will most likely move at a somewhat slower pace. This does not mean that you will not be able to accomplish anything – just that loose ends must be tied up now in order to clear the way for future action, instead of letting them accumulate.

18 MONDAY There seems to be an emphasis on education, long-distance travelling and foreigners. It may very well be that you are attracted to those who come from foreign lands, and you'll be learning a good deal then, and your experience will widen considerably.

19 TUESDAY The planetary set-up today indicates other people and matters are unlikely to be moving quickly enough to please you. Irritating as this snail's pace approach may be, you could find that you accomplish more by it than by tackling matters at a faster, but perhaps less efficient, rate.

20 WEDNESDAY As matters over the past few days have clearly illustrated, it is sometimes wiser to just go along with what other people want, or insist is right. By waiting until the dust has settled, most likely in a few days you'll be able to interject reason into a situation that could otherwise have been explosive.

21 THURSDAY All of us hear the phrase 'it's a matter of opinion' but recently events have amply illustrated this meaning in your life. You may still be reeling from the shock of learning what others believe or insist is true, but it is entirely a matter of opinion and there's absolutely nothing you can do right now, except be complacent.

22 FRIDAY Giving advice is easy, but letting other people make their own mistakes shows understanding and wisdom. It may be difficult to maintain your silence during a crisis that may recently have occurred and which probably affected those closest to you, but their resulting trust is worth it.

23 SATURDAY You seem to be coming to your senses as far as emotional attachments are concerned and you can now tie up a number of loose ends and say goodbye to certain individuals without feeling any trace of guilt or remorse. This, of course, will leave you free to concentrate on people who have your best interests at heart.

24 SUNDAY Today's aspects indicate that you should be enjoying yourself. This is not a time, then, for sitting glued to the television. It is unlikely that you could do this for more than a few minutes anyway. Go out and find the activities that enable you to use up that energy of yours and meet as many new people as possible. Important romantic developments could occur at this time.

25 MONDAY There are many intriguing opportunities for change and yet you hesitate. Perhaps it is just that you are waiting for exactly the right one? Or is it your famous pride that is leading some kind of doubt and self-criticism, which makes you anxious about making the right choice? This is a time for taking out your bravery and dusting it down. Be bold.

26 TUESDAY Right now no sign is going to benefit more from their intellect than yours, yet there are occasions when those crisp thoughts, usually your allies, can undermine you. The stars emphasize the importance of paying attention to what you sense and feel when you make decisions, particularly those involving your own emotions and feelings of other people.

27 WEDNESDAY Those in close relationships will find that they are running much more smoothly and the complications of the past may drift into the mists of time. No doubt this will make you heave a sigh of relief and who can blame you.

28 THURSDAY This is the day of the Full Moon and it occurs in the earthy sign of Taurus and the section of your chart devoted to money matters. It's a good time for nailing down any outstanding quibbles over finances, but don't be tempted to lay down the law with your bank manager. Confidence is fine, but he or she won't be in the mood to be bullied.

29 FRIDAY An insight into an event related to health or an ongoing responsibility will enable you to make arrangements which are long overdue. However, don't assume that close associates will be totally responsive or supportive, because they have other matters on their mind.

♈

30 SATURDAY Right now Venus is very much entrenched in the sign of Libra which, of course, is your opposite number and so all of your relationships are going to be much more smooth from hereon in. There's an awful lot to look forward to so push ahead and those of you who are getting engaged or married couldn't have picked a better time.

31 SUNDAY The month ends on a reasonably good note: there's pleasant news from friends who happen to be abroad and lots of chances for you to enjoy yourself during this particular day and also, perhaps, tomorrow. Don't be too picky or too arrogant, give as much as you can in all areas – and we're not talking money here – and all should be well.

NOVEMBER

The Sun this month will be swimming along in the water sign of Scorpio until the 21st, and that's the area of your chart devoted to big business, club activities, friendship and contacts. However, don't always insist on getting your own way, because if you do I'm afraid you could come a cropper one way or the other.

On the 22nd, the Sun will be moving into Sagittarius, which is the area of your chart devoted to matters related to abroad, so if you have any friends in distant lands they're likely to be getting in touch with you. Furthermore, those of you taking any kind of examination or test are likely to be lucky, so control any feelings of inadequacy because, let's face it, you're as good as anybody else, remember that.

Mercury will be in Scorpio for the first couple of days and if you have anyone in your life born under this sign that's the person to go to for some kind of advice. On the 5th, this particular planet will be moving into Sagittarius where it stays for the remainder of the month, so once more there is an emphasis on higher education, matters related to abroad and import/export matters. All of these should run smoothly so get out your confidence and dust it down.

Venus will be in Libra until the 22nd and that, of course, is your opposite sign, so the emphasis is on your relationships. Those of you who have decided to become engaged or married at this time have certainly picked an ideal period for doing just that.

On the 23rd, Venus will be moving into Scorpio, and the area of your chart devoted to banking matters, big business, and your relationships with workmates and contacts. You've precious little to worry about here.

Mars will be in Libra until 10 November when it moves on into Scorpio. As Libra is your opposite sign, it will mean that other people could be tetchy, bad tempered and unwilling to cooperate with you, so don't expect too much from them, or else you will be sadly disappointed.

The pattern made by the stars indicates that once more there's a hard-working time ahead. You don't mind working to deadlines but you must also look after your health and rest up from time to time. You need to take care of your finances too, as Christmas isn't far away.

1 MONDAY Today will bring minor changes where work matters are concerned with perhaps new workmates figuring prominently. If it is necessary for you to sign any professional contracts over the next few days or so, then you have an ideal time for doing just that.

2 TUESDAY Your outlook is better than it has been for some time but there are still improvements which can be made to your finances. Now with the stars urging a different approach, you can afford to set your sights further afield. An overseas external influence will be more controlled than you're prepared to allow – it's up to you to find the strategy which will achieve your immediate aims without impairing long-term ambitions.

3 WEDNESDAY A romantic creative dream can now be put on a realistic footing, provided allowances have been made for those on the periphery. You're likely to be single-minded about pursuing your goals but just remember that what you want is not necessarily what others seek, and that there is more to be gained just now through compromise than coercion.

4 THURSDAY What occurs today will change the basis of an important relationship. This is something you have been preparing for – deliberately or subconsciously – for some time and the outcome should be positive and productive. Don't exert or over-pressurize yourself.

5 FRIDAY A simmering domestic or family issue is about to reach boiling point and you need to be very clear about what you hope to accomplish. With several planets in difficult aspects even sincerely held views are liable to be misconstrued. Don't mistake intense feelings for fact when dealing with a delicate issue. Nor should you expect others to read your mind when you scarcely know what is driving it yourself.

6 SATURDAY It may be a good idea to adopt a more cynical attitude towards yourself today. You will be changing your mood on the hour, every hour of the day. Confused? How do you think other people feel? Because of this mood it might not be a good idea to commit yourself to anything which requires intense concentration. Busy yourself with putting the finishing touches to already-started jobs or chores.

7 SUNDAY A new relationship or romance may get off to a bad or slow start, but this will gradually improve with time, provided you are prepared to persevere. However, you may decide to pack the whole thing in and look elsewhere. After all, you can't be bothered with those who seem to be sent only to hassle you. What's more, you could be right.

8 MONDAY You've reached the climax of a long-running saga involving someone you communicate with on a regular basis. What happens very soon will clarify the situation and may even bring about a solution. Frantic activity over the next couple of days could cause you to invest too much in a project close to your heart. Anyone trying to exert influence on your personal life should be swiftly discouraged.

9 TUESDAY Today is geared towards group activity or team work, and you must be careful not to overdo it. In fact, the planetary activity suggests that demands upon you are likely to increase over the next few days or so. You'll be firing on all cylinders and must be careful to keep events in a true perspective.

10 WEDNESDAY This could either be the start of something big or a firework which fails to explode. The stars today signify an opening or an opportunity, but it is your actions that will dictate the eventual outcome. The potential for misunderstanding is still high, so don't put anything in writing.

♈

11 THURSDAY An influential figure is willing to help you out but you must first be committed to helping yourself; once they see that you're willing to do this they'll be on your side.

12 FRIDAY This is a good time for attending to health matters, and also for going out of your way to help other people. Should you be asked to become involved in a charity, then accept, as you will find it a learning and fulfilling experience.

13 SATURDAY Something is about to occur which could have an important effect on your financial life. The planetary action is clearing a way for changes during the next couple of days, but much relies upon your input. This is not a time for speculation or making grandiose gestures, but for knuckling down to what has to be done.

14 SUNDAY You seem to be looking at filling a gap in your life but there appears to be conflict between your ambitions and your strong sense of duty. Right now the temptation will be to use delaying tactics, but you have reached a point when you must take a chance and accept that your own needs cannot always take second place. Besides, the same door seldom opens twice.

15 MONDAY There's a shift in emphasis, perhaps even a separation is likely, and there are people who need to be kept informed. Today's aspects suggest that something you have been working towards is about to reach fruition. Avoid finalizing matters for a couple of days because you have too much going on to risk losing everything due to an oversight.

16 TUESDAY As an Aries, you can be unwisely impatient and this leads to injuries, whether they be minor or even major. With today's current planetary aspects, providing you are careful you have precious little to worry about.

17 WEDNESDAY You're beginning a period of intense hard work which, although exhausting, you will find exhilarating as well as profitable in the long run. This is a time for allowing those who count to know exactly what to expect with your job and hopefully they will respect you for doing so.

18 THURSDAY You may not be able to figure out what other people are up to, whether their plans are something that you should worry about or perhaps you are just blowing everything out of proportion. Either way, there will be some changes around you at this time but they will work in your favour.

19 FRIDAY This is not an ideal time to be too critical with loved ones otherwise their flare ups could ruin your day, which would be a pity. Choose your time carefully before making any kind of comment about their behaviour.

20 SATURDAY You step out of character and seem to be reining in partners and keeping them from making commitments that promise little in the way of return. But now they have become interested in a practical or financial matter, and it is their questions that have put certain dubious projects in perspective.

21 SUNDAY There's a certain amount of upheaval and change in connection with the friendship area of your chart. If you've made arrangements with people who live close by, it might be a good idea to do some double checking, because influences beyond their control may stop them from keeping a promise to you.

22 MONDAY Today you need to take care what you say because it might be misinterpreted. If you are foolish enough to confide what is supposed to be a secret, then I'm afraid it will be broadcast around and you'll finish up with a red face.

23 TUESDAY There are occasions when situations themselves seem determined to make up for past problems or ways in which you were unjustly treated. You should now trust to instinct and unexpected circumstances and things that were unfair will be changed into something far more just and rewarding.

24 WEDNESDAY There's a strong chance that you may spend unwisely or impulsively. Do try to think before you buy – better still, get others to shop for you. You may be trusted to buy the odd loaf of bread, but anything more ambitious could be a source of loss.

25 THURSDAY This may be a time when it will be necessary for you to accept changing conditions within the family. It may also be a time when you are expected to accept added responsibility and make commitments. There are no instant solutions to this and you shouldn't allow yourself to be pushed or pressured in any way, shape or form. It may be necessary for you to do a little homework or research before you can decide what needs to be done in this direction.

26 FRIDAY There are occasions when situations themselves seem determined to make up for past problems or ways in which you were unjustly treated. However, if you trust to instinct unexpected circumstances that were once unfair will now become far more welcome and pleasurable. Today's Full Moon in Gemini definitely brings to an end one longstanding wrangle.

27 SATURDAY Not even the most generous approach can overcome a rigid and uncooperative attitude, so if you have done all that you can you may just call it a day. Of course, this by no means indicates you are giving up on things, only that you are waiting for others to see the light.

28 SUNDAY The stars suggest you are taking up an unexpected opportunity, trying to complete a new task. It could revolutionize your life, not only now, but also in terms of what you regard as possible for the future.

29 MONDAY Although you may be aware of the fact that other people are being non-committal and evasive, this probably isn't the right moment to start issuing ultimatums or making threats. If you want to achieve your ambitions, it will be necessary for you to exercise restraint.

30 TUESDAY Just because matters connected with cash or other practical areas of life seem in a bit of disarray and confusion, there really isn't any reason to worry about life in general. Quite the opposite in fact, as there may be no better time for reorganizing, reviewing and, perhaps even more importantly, throwing out a great deal of clutter which has been a source of difficulty and frustration.

DECEMBER

The Sun this month will be sizzling its way through the fiery sign of Sagittarius up until the 21st and that is, of course, the area of your chart devoted to long distance travelling, foreign contacts, higher education and all matters related to abroad. There's likely to be some exciting news from people who are old friends though you may not have heard from them for quite some time, so there's plenty to look forward to.

On the 22nd, the Sun will be moving into Capricorn, and this is the zenith point of your chart. Therefore it looks as if you're 'one pointed' where work matters are concerned and nobody is going to tread on your toes – you're going to see to that, that is for sure. But during your ruthless path up to the top, for heaven's sake be a little bit careful, because we often meet the same people on your way down as on your way up and you really don't want to make enemies.

Mercury is in retrograde action so it's not a good time for signing documents, well not until the 19th anyway when this planet decides to see some kind of sense. After this you can push ahead.

Venus is in Scorpio for the first half of this month before it slips into Sagittarius, emphasizing matters related to friends, club activities and contacts too. Some of you may even be meeting an exciting new foreigner if you happen to be fancy free. If you're not free, however, my advice to you is to be a little bit careful: you could be found out in no uncertain fashion.

Mars will be in Scorpio until the 25th, and so this is not a time to take liberties with the law or your bosses and seniors on the working front. You don't want to make any kind of enemies at this time, and if you do I'm afraid you will regret it in no uncertain fashion. Always remember, Aries, that you are

Monthly and Daily Guides: December

the sort of person who leaps into action in all areas without thinking first and it's about time you learnt that this is no way to travel; if you can do that all should be well. The pattern made by the stars indicates that during December there may be several changes either on the working front or in home life too. Again finances are highlighted because, let's face it, December is probably the most expensive month of the year – one to be enjoyed, of course, but you don't want to face the start of next year having to meet up with your bank manager.

1 WEDNESDAY Today the stars don't seem to bode well for your love life because the chances are that you have become detrimentally involved with the opposite sex. You may be attracted to somebody who is already married or already has a partner. Just ask yourself whether this is worthwhile and why, and I think you'll find the answer is 'no'.

2 THURSDAY Finely tuned intuitions are certainly working near to perfection, especially where money matters are concerned, and so it's important that you concentrate on the practicalities. It is likely that you've learnt that the best way to go forward is to be unhindered and free to move, so you'll trim down your lifestyle accordingly in order to get the maximum results with the minimum of effort. You're really fired up and your determination to reach your goals this time should mean you'll be successful.

3 FRIDAY You'd better make the most of any time for yourself because what you discover in contemplation will be of great value. This may be a quiet day, giving you time to evaluate what has taken place recently. There are many changes and not all of them to your liking. Ask yourself what needs to be changed now to make the future more exciting.

4 SATURDAY There's an opportunity that you can put some of your ideas into practice. How successful you are relies on the finding of the correct balance between reality and theory. It's one thing to know what needs to be done, but quite another to find the right way of doing it. A bit of thought will take you a long way.

5 SUNDAY It's a perfect time for assessing where you have come in life to date and where you wish to go in future. Think long and hard before committing yourself to changes in a job, home or outlook, as you will need to bear the consequences for some time to come. Also avoid becoming involved with members of the opposite sex who are already spoken for.

6 MONDAY This morning you'll simply not have time to fit everything in which needs attention, therefore, slow down and spread your activities over the entire day instead of attempting to solve everything in a matter of hours. You have all the time in the world and as an Aries you tend to do better when you slow down your progress, so see what you can do.

7 TUESDAY During this day you must not allow misunderstandings over money make you feel insecure. Have faith in your abilities and judgement and they are likely to be spot on at this time. Paperwork will be important but it's not an ideal time for signing contracts.

8 WEDNESDAY Don't for one moment think you can spend your way out of any kind of difficulty. What is needed now is

Monthly and Daily Guides: December

not a fresh injection of cash, but a new approach to both professional and personal problems. You might even need to shut yourself away from outside influences and think again about the best way to proceed.

9 THURSDAY Look to the future with confidence. A positive attitude today is important, and don't be afraid to press ahead with schemes or plans which have been under consideration for quite a while. You must remember, however, to keep colleagues and loved ones informed of your moods and motives. You want to avoid any serious disagreements – you can't afford anger or to antagonize other people at this stage.

10 FRIDAY The planets suggest you are thinking long and hard on an official matter, or possibly mulling over a contract. If you are in any kind of doubt the best thing to do is to go to the experts. You may be a clever person but you cannot know everything about every subject in the book. Avoid any kind of bluff.

11 SATURDAY Long term prospects are more promising by the day, but short term problems continue. You possess many talents and one of them is not to make an art form out of worrying. Regrettably you cannot push to one side whatever it is that is bothering you because it keeps nagging away at the back of your mind. You just have to confront those who have upset you, even at the risk of creating a scene.

12 SUNDAY The New Moon in fiery Sagittarius means it's an ideal time for tying up loose ends and laying down plans for the next couple of weeks or so. You could not wish for a luckier time for trying for new jobs and setting new objectives for yourself. If you can dream about it, you can also do it. Keep faith with yourself and nothing will be impossible.

13 MONDAY Today the stars suggest that no matter how many times you have knocked on one door in vain, you should try again. In fact, the aspects today suggest that all you have to do in order to get the right answers is to ask the right questions. This is a time when you should decide to boost your reputation and stabilize your finances.

14 TUESDAY Try to strike the right balance between your spiritual and material needs. Above all else, don't allow others' behaviour or financial problems to undermine you. In fact, you should take note of what occurs today because the same situation may happen again in a month's time.

15 WEDNESDAY The stars suggest that tensions have been simmering beneath the surface for quite some time and are about to burst into the open. Try to control yourself for a while because soon the stars will be giving you the green light to make changes – and not only of emphasis but also of scene.

16 THURSDAY You express strong likes and dislikes and there is nothing you dislike more than unexpected change. This is why you really must take advantage of the day in order to overhaul any work pattern on your own terms – what seems to be a good opportunity may turn out to be a distinct advantage.

17 FRIDAY Today you could be picking up bargains. Even better, you're prone to brilliant ideas when it comes to money, so stay alert – there are advantages that are just over the horizon.

Monthly and Daily Guides: December

18 SATURDAY Those of you in steady relationships may finally decide to name the day. For others, there may be an interesting and profitable professional partnership formed.

19 SUNDAY You can expect an opportunity to come your way where a contract is concerned, but if it becomes necessary for you to sign on the dotted line you'd better procrastinate for a week or so; that way things will go well for you.

20 MONDAY Today there seems to be a certain amount of wishful thinking going on and this is likely to be due to the fact that you are avoiding the truth concerning a situation. The reality of the matter is that your chart at the moment is confused and uncertain. In fact, you appear to be recovering from surprises that occurred a couple of days ago. Take time before making emotional commitments.

21 TUESDAY This is a particularly good time for those of you involved in banking, the stock exchange, or big business. It's also good for other Rams who wish to deal with such people and in these areas you can afford to push ahead with confidence in the knowledge that you're doing the right thing. Do not allow yourself to be intimidated by anybody.

22 WEDNESDAY It's an ideal time for dealing with legal matters and foreign affairs, or long-distance travel. It's a good time, too, for those whose work depends on inspiration and creativity and in this area you are unbeatable and should push ahead with both rivals and competitors. This evening you need stimulating company.

23 THURSDAY A career or professional change is certainly suggested even though the actual move itself cannot be put into operation until later on. No doubt there will be the odd moment when you feel uncertain or out of sorts, but on no account allow self-doubt or, worse, self-pity to creep in.

24 FRIDAY Today, of course, is Christmas Eve and no doubt you are rushed off your feet. If you have a family, of course, this is an enchanting time. Make sure that your arrangements are firing on all cylinders, and then you can enjoy yourself teasing the children about Father Christmas!

25 SATURDAY MERRY CHRISTMAS. Hopefully this is going to be a wonderful day for you. Don't be surprised if one or two strangers pop in to see you. Unlike some signs who may be put out by this, you're quite happy to open your doors to anybody and they will be feeling the benefit of your warm welcome.

26 SUNDAY Boxing Day of course, is usually far more relaxed than the hurly-burly and rush that led up to Christmas. It's quite possible, however, that the old telephone is going to be white hot with invitations for the New Year and you will be delighted to know that you've got plenty of choices to choose from as to where you're going to go and who you're going to see.

27 MONDAY This is a bit of a quiet day. Possibly your children, if you have any, may be a little bit upset, tummy-wise rather than anything else. If so mollycoddle them and in no time at all they will recover, you can be quite sure of that.

Monthly and Daily Guides: December

28 TUESDAY It looks as if you'll be hearing from those friends that you have abroad and this will delight you no end. Furthermore, they may be announcing that they are visiting your shores at some point and this will really please and delight you.

29 WEDNESDAY Some of you may have to go back to work, which is a bit of a bind. Nevertheless, for many of you, you'll be quite happy for a change of pace; things have been rather quiet recently and now you can't wait to get back in the reins of the working front.

30 THURSDAY Surprise visitors may drop in. These may only be neighbours who are perhaps a little bit bored watching the old television, but whoever it is will find a warm welcome waiting for them. Your partner, too, will rally around and help you out if there's any cooking to be done.

31 FRIDAY New Year's Eve and no doubt you've got millions of invitations to choose from for how you're going to enjoy yourself. Get out into the big wide world and make the most of life before the New Year arrives.

HAPPY NEW YEAR

Your Birth Chart by Teri King

A Book of Life

Simply fill in your details on the form below for an interpretation of your birth chart compiled by TERI KING. Your birth chart will be supplied bound and personalized. Each chart costs £40.00 Sterling – add £2.50 Sterling for postage if you live outside the UK (US Dollars are not accepted). Cheques should be made payable to *Kingstar* and sent together with your form to: PO Box 3444, Brighton, East Sussex, BN1 4BX, England. For all *Kingstar* enquiries contact bright77_@hotmail.com.

Date of Birth _____ Place of Birth _____

Time of Birth _____

Country of Birth _____

Name (in BLOCK CAPITALS) _____

Address _____

_____

_____ Postcode _____

Email _____

A birth chart makes an ideal present. On a separate sheet, why not include the details of a friend, partner or a member of your family? Please see the above costs for each individual chart.

Make www.thorsonselement.com your online sanctuary

Get online information, inspiration and guidance to help you on the path to physical and spiritual well-being. Drawing on the integrity and vision of our authors and titles, and with health advice, articles, astrology, tarot, a meditation zone, author interviews and events listings, www.thorsonselement.com is a great alternative to help create space and peace in our lives.

So if you've always wondered about practising yoga, following an allergy-free diet, using the tarot or getting a life coach, we can point you in the right direction.

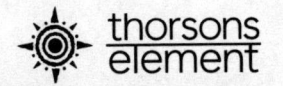

thorsons element